CHRISTIANS IN THE PUBLIC SQUARE: FAITH IN PRACTICE?

Richard D. Land
& Lee Hollaway
Editors

ERLC PUBLICATIONS

NASHVILLE, TENNESSEE

© 1996
by the Christian Life Commission
of the Southern Baptist Convention

Published in Nashville, Tennessee,
by ERLC Publications, a subsidiary of
the Christian Life Commission
of the Southern Baptist Convention.

All rights reserved.
Written permission must be secured
from the publisher for use or reproduction
of any part of this book except for
brief quotations in critical reviews or articles.

Cover design by Ernie Hickman

Richard D. Land & Lee Hollaway (eds.)
Christians in the Public Square:
Faith in Practice?

ISBN 1-888880-01-5

Religion. Current affairs.
Library of Congress Card Number: 96-84947

1 2 3 4 5 000 99 98 97 96

Preface

From the perspective of these final days of the millennium, one might well characterize the twentieth century as the "secular century." An inflated sense of human potential has prompted humankind increasingly to explore its own direction, with a declining regard for divine directives.

Unquestionably humanity has achieved some remarkable successes in the past century, especially in the fields of transportation, communication, and medical science. We have explored the moon and beyond, and reduced the distance between individuals to milliseconds. The record, however, is far different when attention is focused on moral issues. The twentieth century has been the most violent in recorded history, from Auschwitz and Dachau and the tens of millions of victims murdered by Soviet and Chinese communism to the more recent extermination of millions of unborn babies.

The neat, frame churches that were the center of community life at the beginning of this century have in many cases been left to decay by the side of the road. Where they remain, their role has largely been preempted by everything from television to Little League. Many people still go to church, but it is just one of a dozen or more activities that fill their weekly schedule.

In recent years Christian leaders have been reminded pointedly that the diminished role of religion in American life has occurred to a significant degree by default. The failure of Christians to take a proactive stance on critical issues—indeed, their tacit withdrawal from, or neglect of, the public square—created a vacuum that other interests did not hesitate to fill.

Evangelical Christians give increasing evidence of having learned from their previous error. Within the past decade they have begun to rediscover the dynamics of political life and let their voices be heard on a variety of issues. They have reentered the public square, sometimes with a vengeance, seeking to compensate for years of silence and neglect. Far fewer believers now challenge the legitimacy of either a corporate or individual public role for Christians in the nation's public life.

One critical question remains, however: On what terms should Christian public-policy involvement proceed? What approaches will maximize Christian impact for righteousness within the culture without sacrificing the historic Christian witness? As one of the writers in this volume points out, the fundamental issue for citizen Christians is not so much "how" as "why." Is our participation in the public square truly a reflection of our faith put into practice?

Each of the contributors to this volume has approached this matter from his or her own unique background of experience. They originally shared their thoughts during the 29th annual national seminar sponsored by the Christian Life Commission of the Southern Baptist Convention, held in Washington, D.C., on March 4-6, 1996. They have graciously consented to have their ideas shared with a wider audience through this book.

Special thanks go to Edith Wilson, the CLC's editorial assistant, for efficiently preparing the chapter manuscripts for final production.

We pray that God will use this book to help enlighten both Southern Baptists and non-Southern Baptists about the importance of properly motivated and Holy Spirit-guided involvement in the public square.

Lee Hollaway
Richard D. Land
Nashville, Tennessee

Contents

Preface iii
Contributors vii
Introduction ix

OUR PLACE IN THE SQUARE

Will It Be Faith in Practice?
   by Richard D. Land 1

God's Universal Standard
   by Mark E. Dever 9

Ten Commandments for Christian Citizens
   by Charles G. Fuller 23

America: An Ecotonic Moment in Time
   by O. S. Hawkins 29

Being Salt and Light in America
   by Gary Bauer 43

CHALLENGES WE FACE

When Christians Don't Make a Difference
   by David P. Gushee 53

The Fight for Religious Liberty
   by Jay Sekulow 67

Being Salt in an Unsavory World: The Spiritual Cancer of Pornography and How to Fight It
   by Dee A. Jepsen 81

The Christian, the Media, and the Issues
   by Gary Ledbetter 95

MAKING A SIGNIFICANT DIFFERENCE

Have You Got Good Religion?
by Gary Frost................................. 103

Pastors For Life: Mobilizing for Spiritual Leadership
by Michael Cloer 115

Engaging the Local Public Square
by Daniel R. Heimbach 123

Transforming the Black Church in Suburbia
by E. W. McCall, Sr.......................... 129

Hope for the Hurting
by Charles Roesel 139

Contributors

Gary Bauer is president of the Family Research Council, a pro-family policy and lobbying group based in Washington, D.C. Before joining the FRC in 1988, he was a member of President Ronald Reagan's White House staff and also had spent four years in the U.S. Department of Education.

Michael Cloer has been pastor of Siloam Baptist Church, located in Powdersville, on the outskirts of Easley, S.C., for more than eight years. He is also the founder and director of Pastors For Life, a pro-life organization which seeks to encourage pastor involvement in the movement.

Mark Dever became pastor of Capitol Hill Baptist Church, Washington, D.C., in 1994 after earning a Ph.D. in ecclesiastical history at Cambridge University in England.

Gary Frost is pastor of Rising Star Baptist Church, Youngstown, Ohio. He was second vice-president of the Southern Baptist Convention in 1994-95 and 1995-96.

Charles Fuller has been pastor of First Baptist Church, Roanoke, Va., since 1961. He has held numerous state and national denominational positions, including that of chairman of the Southern Baptist Convention Peace Committee, 1985-88.

David Gushee is assistant professor of Christian ethics at the Southern Baptist Theological Seminary, Louisville, Ky. He formerly was on the staff of Evangelicals for Social Action.

O. S. Hawkins is pastor of the 25,000-member First Baptist Church, Dallas, Tex. He also has been president of the Southern Baptist Pastors' Conference.

Dan Heimbach is associate professor of Christian ethics at the Southeastern Baptist Theological Seminary, Wake Forest, N.C. He also holds elected office as a town commissioner for the town of Wake Forest. He spent three years on the staff of Senator Richard Lugar of Indiana and two years on the White House staff of President George Bush.

Dee Jepsen is national president and a major spokesperson for the "Enough is Enough!" anti-pornography campaign, based in Fairfax, Va. She was a special assistant to President Ronald Reagan as liaison between women's organizations and the White House. Her husband, Roger Jepsen, was formerly a U.S. Senator from Iowa.

Richard D. Land is president and chief executive officer of the Southern Baptist Christian Life Commission, with offices in Nashville, Tenn., and Washington, D.C. He came to this social and moral concerns agency in 1988, having served previously as vice-president for academic affairs at Criswell College in Dallas, Texas, and as administrative assistant to the governor of Texas.

Gary Ledbetter became vice-president for student development at Midwestern Baptist Theological Seminary in Kansas City, Mo., in December, 1995. Prior to that he had been editor since 1989 of the *Indiana Baptist,* newsjournal of the State Convention of Baptists in Indiana. He was chairman of the Southern Baptist Christian Life Commission in 1994-95.

E. W. McCall has been pastor of St. Stephen Missionary Baptist Church, LaPuente, Calif., since 1970. He is also president of the California Southern Baptist African American Network and president of the national African American Fellowship.

Charles Roesel has been pastor of First Baptist Church, Leesburg, Fla., for more than 19 years. During that time the church has grown to more than 6,000 members, had more than 4,000 baptisms, and started more than 50 separate ministries in its community.

Jay Sekulow is chief litigator for the American Center for Law and Justice, Washington, D.C. In that capacity he has argued numerous church-state cases before the United States Supreme Court.

Introduction

By Richard D. Land

The essays comprising the chapters in this volume were first delivered orally by their authors during the Southern Baptist Christian Life Commission's 29th annual seminar in Washington, D.C., March 4-6, 1996. The seminar's theme, "Christians in the Public Square: Faith in Practice?" sought to address the question of the Christian's role in the nation's public life and to examine the extent to which such participation was, or could be, a legitimate expression of religious faith and practice.

In a very real sense, the seminar speakers wrestled with the issues raised by Christian participation in American society as they are articulated in the *Baptist Faith and Message* confession of faith approved by vote of the Southern Baptist Convention in 1963. *The Baptist Faith and Message's* articles on "The Christian and the Social Order" and on "Religious Liberty" illustrate the tensions involved whenever Christians in the "free church" tradition contemplate their responsibilities to be "salt" and "light" in society while being faithful at the same time to the long-cherished commitment to religious liberty and the separation of the institutions of church and state.

Jesus has commanded Christians to be the "salt" of the earth and the "light" of the world (Matt. 5:13-16). Obedience to this divine command will involve Christians in active engagement with the world, preserving as "salt" and illuminating as "light." Involvement in society is not optional if being salt and light is the Christian's goal.

The Baptist Faith and Message affirms this call to involvement with the world when it states under "The Christian and the Social Order" that "every Christian is under obligation to seek to make the will of Christ supreme in his own life and in human society." *The Baptist Faith and Message* also says that Christians not only "should oppose, in the spirit of Christ every form of greed, selfishness, and vice," but "should seek to bring industry, government, and society as a whole under the sway of the principles of righteousness, truth, and brotherly love."

Introduction

At the same time *The Baptist Faith and Message's* statement on "Religious Liberty" proclaims a "free church in a free state is the Christian ideal" and that "the church should not resort to the civil power to carry on its work" for the "gospel of Christ contemplates spiritual means alone for the pursuit of its ends."

Is there an inevitable conflict or tension between the Christian's obligation to be salt and light and the Christian's responsibility to advocate and practice religious liberty? This is the question with which this volume's authors wrestled and sought to address. In the first chapter I ask the question, "Will It Be Faith in Practice?" I concluded that it can and should be so, but "only if Christians understand fully that their ultimate allegiance and obedience belong to Christ alone" and that "We must never sell the birthright of our second birth to any human leader, to any political party, or to any social movement."

Next, we hear from three local church pastors, men who stand on the front lines of spiritual conflict every week as they seek to shepherd their local assemblies of believers and to reach the lost in their communities amidst the challenges and conflicts of the twentieth century's last decade. *Mark Dever* uses the Old Testament prophet Obadiah's message in clever and thought-provoking ways to challenge Christians to think "theologically" about God's truth and the fact that God does have a "universal standard" by which He judges men and nations.

Charles Fuller surveys the nation's moral crisis and proclaims that "Christians have a rightful place in the public square." He then uses 1 Peter 2:11-17 to formulate "Ten Commandments for Christian Citizens" which every Christian would profit from pondering thoughtfully and prayerfully.

O.S. Hawkins finds startling and disturbing parallels between the moral and spiritual crises which confronted the Old Testament prophet Jeremiah and the crises which American Christians face today. Dr. Hawkins echoes the lament of Jeremiah that "my people know not the judgment of the Lord" (Jer. 8:7) and, like Jeremiah, calls God's people to come back in repentance and humility to God.

Gary Bauer contrasts the tremendous and awe-inspiring achievements of American civilization in the twentieth century with the present "virtue deficit this country increasingly wrestles with" and challenges American Christians to be salt and light. He then defines what is at stake: "Unless men and women of faith get into the public square and stand for certain values, America will fall as surely as it would from economic collapse."

Introduction

In the section entitled "Challenges We Face" *David Gushee* explains in tragic detail what happens in a society "When Christians Don't Make a Difference." Using the rise of Nazism in Germany as his example, Gushee chronicles the failure of German Christians to oppose, and in some cases, their willingness to support, the Nazi goals and agenda. Gushee's narrative of the failures of German Christians, liberal and conservative, to make a difference in bearing a Gospel witness against Hitler should serve as a cautionary tale to any and all who would seek to wed a particular ideology to the Gospel as well as to those who would urge Christians to withdraw from their citizenship responsibilities.

Jay Sekulow, fresh from courtroom confrontations in his role as chief litigator for the American Center for Law and Justice, argues eloquently for Christians to demand their historical and proper role as full participants in American public policy debate and reminds us that Martin Luther King, Jr's "Letter From the Birmingham City Jail" declared that "just law is a man-made code that squares with the moral law or the law of God." Sekulow's call to engagement and proposed plan of action will challenge every Christian to think long and hard about the issues he raises and the solutions he suggests.

Dee Jepsen addresses one of the gravest and most serious problems plaguing American society today—pornography. A frontline warrior against this spiritual evil, Jepsen surveys the devastating effects of pornography both on the men addicted to its vile and twisted view of human sexuality and on the women and children who become their victims. Using the lessons learned in leading the very successful "Enough is Enough!" campaign against pornography, Jepsen explains how Christians can make a real difference to stop, and even to roll back, the pornographic tide that threatens to engulf our society.

If Christians are to penetrate American culture with biblical truth with any degree of success, they must deal with and utilize the media far more effectively than they have heretofore. In "The Christian, the Media, and the Issues" *Gary Ledbetter* furnishes a persuasive apologetic for seeking to engage the media for just such goals and purposes. While candidly acknowledging the potential down side to such interaction with the media, Ledbetter points out that if Christians are well-prepared and articulate, they can use the media to propogate Christian truths to a far wider spectrum of their fellow Americans than would otherwise be possible. Ledbetter's extremely helpful guidelines for dealing with the

Introduction

media compress a wealth of experience and information into a compact, usable body of information. Christians who employ these guidelines will maximize their impact and minimize their mistakes in interacting with the media.

Turning again to local pastors and leadership, **Gary Frost** asks Christians if they have "good" religion, and then employs the first twelve verses of the fifty-eighth chapter of Isaiah's prophecy to distinguish between the wrong (vv. 1-5) and the right (vv. 6-7) reasons for religion. Frost then summarizes that "good" religion "fights injustice," "seeks to break bondages," and "responds to poverty." His challenge to seek "good" religion will help all Christians and their churches move closer to Christ's ideal for His church.

Michael Cloer's ministry in defense of the unborn in America illustrates just how much difference pastoral leadership dedicated to truth and righteousness can make both in local communities and across the nation. Pastor Cloer shares his vision and experiences in seeking to call pastors across America to provide spiritual leadership in the struggle to preserve precious unborn human life. Like so many of us, Cloer believes abortion on demand is the single greatest moral failure of American democracy in our lifetime, and it will only be reduced when the churches of America are convicted and mobilized against this monstrous evil. Michael Cloer's challenge to make a difference for life should cause all of us to reevaluate our commitment and to ask ourselves, "Am I doing all I can and should be doing to stop the killing of babies in their mother's wombs?"

Dan Heimbach furnishes us with an inspiring example of how God has called one Christian to make a difference by standing for truth in the public policy arena by running for elective public office. Heimbach relates how God led him to run for, and be elected, a town commissioner in Wake Forest, North Carolina, where he serves on the faculty of Southeastern Baptist Theological Seminary. Heimbach also tells of his successful efforts, along with other concerned town folk in Wake County, to construct and implement a character education program in the county's public schools which "focused on eight character traits: courage, good judgment, integrity, kindness, perseverance, respect, responsibility, and self-discipline." Heimbach's successful impact on the local public square should inspire Christians everywhere to make a difference in the communities where they live, work, worship, and rear their families.

Introduction

E.W. McCall brings his wealth of pastoral experience and expertise to the subject of how to transform the black church in suburban settings. The principles he outlines for implementing such a transformation are provocative and comprehensive. Any local church would find them most helpful in reaching and impacting their local communities, whatever their ethnic or social setting.

Charles Roesel tells the inspiring story of how God transformed a traditional Southern Baptist church in the midst of complacency and on the edge of decline into a vibrant fellowship of believers who are impacting their community from top to bottom in imaginative and life-transforming ways. As Roesel put it, "Many would have said, 'Nothing significant can happen in a church like First Baptist of Leesburg.' But I repeat: Any place will do if God is in the place and any preacher will do if God is in the preacher." Charles Roesel's experience in Leesburg should inspire all of us to lift our eyes to the Lord from whence cometh our strength (Ps. 18:2; 27:1) and then look around us to the fields "white already to harvest" (John 4:35) and, without setting limits or conditions, ask God what He would have each of us do right where we live.

Our Place
In the Square

WILL IT BE FAITH IN PRACTICE?

By Richard D. Land

The theme for the Christian Life Commission's 29th Annual Seminar is "Christians in the Public Square: Faith in Practice?" That question mark is of vital significance. The Scripture verse that accompanies the theme is Proverbs 14:34: *"Righteousness exalteth a nation: but sin is a reproach to any people."* This is a powerful and important verse for the day and time in which we live. To illustrate how this verse applies to the theme, think about the following passage from the Book of Jeremiah. Jeremiah was written during the last days of Judah's idolatry and sin before Judah was carried off into Babylonian captivity. This is what God has Jeremiah say to His people:

> *For from the least of them even unto the greatest of them every one is given to covetousness; and from the prophet even unto the priest every one dealeth falsely. They have healed also the hurt of the daughter of my people slightly, saying, Peace, peace; when there is no peace. Were they ashamed when they had committed abomination? nay, they were not at all ashamed, neither could they blush: therefore they shall fall among them that fall: at the time that I visit them they shall be cast down, saith the Lord. Thus saith the Lord, Stand ye in the ways, and see, and ask for the old paths, where is the good way, and walk therein, and ye shall find rest for your souls. But they said, We will not walk therein. Also I set watchmen over you, saying, Hearken to the sound of*

Christians in the Public Square

the trumpet. But they said, We will not hearken. Therefore hear, ye nations, and know, O congregation, what is among them (Jer. 6:13-18).

We who claim the name of Christian, who claim the identity of being the people of God, need to see ourselves as watchmen and watchwomen who have been put upon the wall to sound the trumpet that *"righteousness does exalt a nation: but sin is a reproach to any people."* We must sound the alarm for the danger is great and the hour is late. "Christians in the Public Square: Faith in Practice?" It can be. It should be. It may be, but it is not guaranteed that it will be faith in practice. It will be faith in practice only if Christians understand fully that our ultimate allegiance and obedience belong to Christ alone.

The Christian Life Commission is very excited about a new book we have just published entitled *Has Democracy Had Its Day?* by Carl F.H. Henry. In this book Dr. Henry addresses this question. He shows how the representative self-government that we call democracy in America is inextricably tied to the basic, fundamental values of a Judeo-Christian world view and that our form of government with the liberties that it guarantees will work only when the vast majority of the people share a common world view and value system that understands as its base that we are going to be accountable to a higher power than mere government. He further shows that a basic belief that people will give an account of their actions and that there are some things that are always right and some things that are always wrong are inextricably intertwined with a Judeo-Christian value system.

Dr. Henry concludes that unless there is a great spiritual awakening and revival in America that is led by people of faith who will then bring that awakening into the public square, there is really no hope for the American nation we have known. Now, the geographic entity that is the United States will almost certainly survive. We will still have the same geographic designations, the same names for towns and cities and valleys and mountain ranges, but the America that we have known, the America that has been bequeathed to us by our ancestors will cease to exist, and we and our children will become strangers in our own land. We will be left to live in an alien America that will be unrecognizable to us as the country we have known and lost.

But why did I say that it may be faith in practice, it should be faith in practice, but it is not guaranteed that it will be faith in practice? In *Has Democracy Had Its Day?* Dr. Henry contrasts his early writing of a half-century ago, *The Uneasy Conscience of*

Will It be Faith in Practice?

Fundamentalism, which called for evangelical Christians to quit existing behind their high walls and to come back into American society and to engage and to seek to transform that society.[1] Indeed, in the past half-century evangelical Christianity "has experienced phenomenal growth."[2] It is arguable that there are more people today in America who would claim an evangelical, born-again faith and personal experience with Jesus Christ as a percentage of the population than at any time in this century. Some have even talked of an "evangelical era." Yet, after a half-century of unprecedented growth among evangelicals, American society, with the exception of discrimination against women and racial minorities, is worse off today than it was a half-century ago in virtually every conceivable way.

Recently I was asked a very interesting question by a reporter. He said, "You have told us about what you are for and what you are against. What would America look like if America were the way you wanted it to be?" I replied, "Well, a good place to start would be America in 1955 without the racism and without the sexual discrimination against women. In 1955 we didn't have a higher percentage of our population in jail than any other country in the world. We do now. In 1955 we weren't aborting one out of every three babies. We are now. Abortion was virtually illegal in every state in every circumstance with the possible exception of the life of the mother.

"We didn't have a homosexual rights movement that was trying to make that particular sin a guaranteed constitutional right. We do now. In fact, homosexuality and lesbianism were considered so perverted that they were not often discussed in polite company. Now, we have school boards trying to tell us that we need to have *Heather Has Two Mommies* and *Heather Goes to Gay Pride* and *Daddy's Roommate* as curriculum in our public schools.

"And a woman wasn't being physically beaten every nine seconds by her husband or by her boyfriend in 1955. They are now. A six-year-old American girl did not have a one in three chance of being sexually molested by her sixteenth birthday, and a six-year-old American boy did not have a one in five chance of being sexually molested by his sixteenth birthday in 1955. They do now. One out of every two marriages didn't end in divorce in 1955. And we didn't have significant percentages of our children being reared in single-parent homes in 1955. The year 1955 was not perfect, but it looks better every day compared to what has come since."

Dr. Henry's point is that after a half-century of Evangelical Christianity being at least as influenced by the secular culture as

Christians in the Public Square

it has impacted that culture, it is not only the society that needs to be transformed, it is the church that must be transformed as well,[3] and the church's transformation must come first. If we are going to have Christians in the public square and it's going to be faith in practice, we must get the faith right first, and it's not faith in a political party. It is not faith in a merely political solution. It is not faith in worldly political power. It is faith first and foremost in Jesus Christ. It is a reliance upon and a trust in the authority of His Word. Our participation in the public square must be accomplished through testing the issues of the day against the litmus test of Christ and His Scripture. What does the Bible have to say about this issue? What would Christ have us do? These must always be our first and most determinative questions.

Now, why is it that we have not been participating as we ought in the public square? One reason is because there are those who guard the public square jealously, and they attack venomously anyone who dares to question them. *The New York Times* has pronounced that public policy advocacy by conservative Evangelical Christians constitutes "a far greater threat to democracy than was presented by communism."[4] Well, at least, we got their attention. In many ways, people who come from the world view presented by the editorial page of *The New York Times* look upon us as alien beings. We might as well be from another planet, not just west of the Hudson. We need to understand that when we challenge their secular, relativist hegemony over American society they will react with outrage and incredulity. We must be prepared to answer their withering criticism and to call it what it is—anti-religious bigotry that seeks to censor us and to keep us from being involved in the public square. Indeed, it is not evangelicals but the narrow, secular biases of the nation's social, political, and media elites (which *The New York Times* symbolizes) that pose a grave threat to American democracy.

When Christians turn to their religious convictions for answers to the moral and spiritual crises that afflict our society they must expect to face harsh criticism. When we bring our moral and religious convictions and our faith affirmations into the public forum of ideas and involve ourselves in the social and political arena, we are exercising our rights as American citizens. The religious convictions of American citizens when they bring them into the public arena are nothing less than the moral concerns of American citizens, which are protected by the First Amendment rights of the Constitution.

Now, it is not just *The New York Times* which has criticized and caricatured evangelical involvement in the public square.

Will It be Faith in Practice?

National Public Radio, which is partially funded by your tax money, had the following statement that came out on December 19, 1995. Andrei Codrescu, a guest commentator from New Orleans, picked up a religious tract outlining a form of a premillennial understanding of the end time which described "the rapture" as "the immediate departure from this earth of over four million people in less than a fifth of a second." Mr. Codrescu then said that as far as he was concerned, "the evaporation of four million people who believe this crap would leave the world an instantly better place." That erudite "commentary" was paid for by your tax money. After a torrent of complaints, NPR issued an apology stating that Codrescu's remarks "crossed a line of taste and tolerance that we should have defended with greater vigilance." Codrescu, however, wasn't quite as contrite, saying that he apologized "for the language, but not for what I said."

Perhaps the most vicious and scandalous attack I have seen in a mainstream American publication appeared in the January 1996 *Gentleman's Quarterly (GQ)*. Entitled "Triumph of His Will," the *GQ* article is a scathing attack on the Promise Keepers movement, one of the most important grass-roots movements to arise in a long time to meet one of the most pressing needs in American life—the need for our male citizens to own up to the consequences of their collective irresponsibility in this culture. This article, written by Scott Raab, compares the Promise Keepers rallies with the Nazi rallies of the 1930s. Raab said that the rally reminded him of nothing more than Leni Riefenstahl's *Triumph of the Will* Nazi propaganda documentary. Raab describes the Promise Keepers' founder, former Colorado football coach Bill McCartney, as "a raving lunatic" and a "lop-eyed loon."[5] In the midst of watching McCartney address a Promise Keepers rally, Raab said "it was impossible not to think of Riefenstahl's documentary *Triumph of the Will*, starring yet another gifted layman, a golden-tongued painter named Adolph."[6] Raab's conclusion is that Evangelical Christians who participate in Promise Keepers are a strange combination of the Nazis, the *Invasion of the Body Snatchers*, and the ayatollah.

If this kind of article had been written about any other group in American society, there would have been a fire storm of controversy. If this vituperative attack had been written about the Black Muslims, for instance, there would have been a tremendous uproar. If this assault had been leveled against any group in America but Evangelical Christians, there would have been an enormous media outcry. But *GQ* refused to apologize for Raab's scurrilous diatribe against Promise Keepers.

Christians in the Public Square

Be prepared to be criticized, and understand that when that criticism comes, it is the price we pay for being obedient to the will of God, because, after all, Jesus said to the Christians, "You are to be the salt of the earth and you are to be the light of the world" (Matt. 5:13-16). Salt is a disinfectant and salt does purify and salt does preserve, but it also stings and burns and irritates. When we come into contact with the world, seeking to be salt, seeking to be a preservative, seeking to be the disinfectant that Jesus commanded us to be, we need to understand that we will be called upon to defend the fact that we irritate and sting and burn those to whom we bear witness.

Jesus says we are to be the light of the world. Light penetrates the darkness, but the Bible tells us that men love darkness rather than light because their deeds are evil. If you shine light into the wrong places, they shoot out your flashlight, and they don't make you the Rotarian of the Year. They say you are a troublemaker. They say you upset the apple cart.

And as we seek to be salt and light, we need to ask ourselves constantly: "Is this position, is this value, is this participation in keeping with the faith that we received from Him?" We must never sell the birthright of our second birth to any human leader, to any political party, or to any social movement. Our allegiance and loyalty belong to Jesus Christ, and it is only as we seek to remain faithful to Him and to understand that what America must have is a revival and a spiritual awakening that lead to a reformation. The revival must come first, the goal being changed people changing the society and changing the world.

Dr. Henry's book has sobered me. First, about how late the hour is—not hopeless, but the hour is late. And second, I had never thought seriously about the fact that the half-century that has witnessed the greatest growth in the history of Evangelicalism in America has also seen the worst moral decay in our nation's history, a decay that is not only outside the church, but has invaded the church and the families of the church and the homes of the church as well.

We must share the gospel, and we must be salt and light, but Jesus said that salt, when it is contaminated is no longer fit for anything except to be thrown out on the road to be trodden underfoot. If we are going to be watchmen on the wall, sounding the trumpet, we must understand that we are His watchmen and we must be pure. We must be unadulterated salt and undimmed light; we must be fit to share and to bear witness to His truth. I pray that all of us will consecrate ourselves to bearing a biblical witness in the public square and will commit ourselves to always

Will It be Faith in Practice?

being eager and willing and striving to understand more and more of what it means to bear a biblical witness so that we can say that the next half-century, if there is another half-century, is not one in which American Christianity grew, but the nation declined and not one in which Christians were influenced as much by society as they managed to influence those around them.

Endnotes

[1] Carl F.H Henry, *Has Democracy Had Its Day?* (Nashville: ERLC Publications, 1996), vii.
[2] Ibid.
[3] Ibid., vii, 51.
[4] "Government Is Not God's Work," *The New York Times*, Aug. 29, 1993.
[5] Scott Raab, "Triumph of His Will," *Gentleman's Quarterly*, January 1996, 113-114.
[6] Ibid., 117.

GOD'S UNIVERSAL STANDARD
The Prophecy of Obadiah*

By Mark E. Dever

Not too long ago, on the phone, I mentioned to a friend that I was to be addressing a meeting on the topic, "What use am I as a theologian?" There was stunned silence on the other side. Then he stammered, sounding almost a little embarrassed, "You consider yourself a theologian?"

All I meant, of course, was that I am a believer who has considered what he believes. Theology simply means words about God, knowledge about God, learning about God. In the sense that human beings are by nature believers, we are all theologians. We all have things which we think about God, whether they're true or false. The only question is, have we articulated them, seen them for what they are, so that we can bring them under the scrutiny of God's Word? But we live in a time too impatient for that.

The only thing that I can say to people on a plane that's more assured to destroy an incipient conversation than "Hello, I'm a Baptist minister" is "Hello, I'm a theologian."

People have some idea of what ministers do, but what do theologians do? Something about angels and pinheads or something?

Even Christian believers are well into the anti-theological mood of our culture. Theologians are apparently open to the ultimate put-down which can be offered up today. It's not to be called "Ichabod," meaning "the glory is departed." It's to be called "impractical," of no use.

*All Scripture references in this chapter are from the New International Version.

Christians in the Public Square

Theologians no longer influence national policy as Cranmer did when telling Henry VIII that he thought he had a pretty good case for a divorce, or as John Leland did when persuading James Madison of the benefits of disestablishment. Most people don't really have strong metaphysical opinions anymore about matters which in the past have torn nations apart.

To the modern secular person, theology is not useful even for giving a credible meaning to life, and so its fortunes are waning; even as the rise of automobiles has made blacksmiths less numerous than they once were, so today, in this enlightened age, aren't theologians really going the same way?

Religion today, when it does intrude into the public sphere, seems to come in only to shore up the agenda which is dictated from other sources, and so politicians on the right and the left exhort the church to do its job, so that we all can live the way we know we should live anyway.

Gertrude Himmelfarb's *The De-Moralization of Society* essentially calls for a "reformation" which "will restore...a more abiding sense of moral and civic virtues" (p. 257). As delightful to Christian ears as her and her husband, Irving Kristol's, calls for moral renewal and spiritual revival are, we must beware a kind of utilitarianism, where the good we seek is only that which is self-evident to humans, entirely apart from the self-revelation of God in Scripture. Even as we can never equate that which is moral with that which is legal, so we can never rely on the children of Adam and Eve to discern the way to please their Creator apart from His own revealing it to us. It is, finally, God who gives meaning and direction to the lives of those creatures He alone has made, and that He alone will judge.

Having said that, though, if we're honest, meaning and significance in our lives may come from many places, but for the overwhelming majority today it has little to do with theology—that is, with knowledge about God.

Well then, it's to an age like ours, to a people like us, that Obadiah, perhaps uniquely among the prophets of the Old Testament, speaks. You see, most of the other prophets speak to Old Testament believers—to us in our churches, rather than to us as public people—but Obadiah proclaims a vision from the sovereign God to people who knew no theology, who had no place for knowledge of God in their lives. He speaks to a society which makes no pretense of acknowledging God. He speaks to a society increasingly like our own.

In this book, God speaks words about Himself to skeptical,

God's Universal Standard

self-sufficient, prosperous people, and He tells them three things:
1. That He will judge them.
2. That He will show concern for a particular people.
3. That He will govern the entire world.

In the end, it turns out that theology—real theology, that is, true knowledge of the real God—is the most practical thing on earth. Let's look at this brief prophecy of Obadiah, as He prophesies God's judgment on the people of Edom, the people who lived just southeast of Judah.

This oracle begins with the announcement that God will judge people for their pride.

The basic situation appears to be that Jerusalem had fallen to the Babylonian invaders, and that these near neighbors, the Edomites, had, to say the least, done nothing to help God's people when they were in their plight. But this little book is not merely the condemnation of an outraged Israelite. In fact, we don't even *know* that Obadiah was an Israelite. We know nothing about Obadiah ["Servant of the Lord"] really; there are twelve different persons of that name alone in the Old Testament, not to mention it simply could have been a descriptive title of this messenger. He had a vision, and it was that vision, from Yahweh, that obed-iyah[weh], servant of Yahweh, proclaims. He brought not his own word, but the Word of God. "This is what the Sovereign LORD says about Edom—We have heard a message from the LORD."

This is basically to say, there is a word for Edom, and the word isn't good.

"An envoy was sent to the nations to say, 'Rise, and let us go against her for battle.'"

Perhaps the rumblings of war were about. It is likely that the Edomites were fearful of invasion by the regional power of the time, the Babylonians, and Obadiah is saying that these rumors of war were not mere scaremongering, but they were warnings that disaster was coming, and that it was coming from God. The nations in mind, it seems, were the nations of the Babylonian empire.

But we don't get the idea that Edom is in any particularly low state when Obadiah delivers this message. In verse 2, Yahweh Himself promises to make Edom "small among the nations; you will be utterly despised." Now this seems to have come as some surprise to them. They weren't aware of any certain doom overhanging them. Perhaps there were some rumors around, but times were good. Their near neighbor Judah had just fallen, and her fall had enriched Edom a bit. They lived in a naturally

Christians in the Public Square

impregnable position, atop mountains, in cities which could be reached only by narrow, winding passages. As I said, they thought that times were good. But look at verse 3:

"The pride of your heart has deceived you," says Yahweh to Edom. "You who live in the clefts of the rocks and make your home on the heights, you who say to yourself, 'Who can bring me down to the ground?'" There was no question that though Edom was a small nation, it was situated, like Switzerland, in an apparently impenetrable region of rocky heights and passes. And their heart, says God, was well symbolized by their terrain—high and hard, certain and proud. But that's where they made their fatal error. In their ability to survey the surrounding country, they thought they could see all, but they couldn't. In the end, God says here, their own pride had deluded them.

In verse 4: "'Though you soar like the eagle and make your nest among the stars, from there I will bring you down,' declares the LORD." God evidently wasn't as impressed with their natural strategic defenses as they were. He recognized no earthly power or advantage that would slow the course of His justice for the slightest moment once He had decided to bring down this proud and boasting people. But the Edomites were mindless of all this. They foolishly relied on their own power, and ignored the sovereign God. As Calvin put it, "It is the greatest madness for men to rely on their own power and to despise God himself."

It is truly amazing to me to see what things people proudly put their trust in. Some will remember, and others will have read, about the famous Maginot Line. From 1929 to 1938, under the directions of the war minister, Andre Maginot, a line of defensive fortifications was constructed along France's border with Germany to avoid a repeat of the disaster of World War I. Thicker concrete, heavier guns, air conditioned rooms with living areas, recreation areas, and even underground railways connecting various strong points of the line—all these things assured the French that they could ignore the German build-up under Hitler. Regardless of the increasing war machine in Germany, the French government was smugly certain they could put their trust in the Maginot Line.

Of course, the only trouble was that when the Germans finally invaded, they came through Belgium, outflanking the Maginot Line, rendering it utterly useless.

We all build our own Maginot Lines, and trust in them. We give obsessive attention to our appearance, our bodies, our possessions, our accomplishments, our reputations, our friendships, trusting them to bring us peace and security. All of

God's Universal Standard

these are things which we can do ourselves, extensions of our own power, reflections of our own ability, declarations of our own proud independence of God. Do you really think those things you trust in to give your life meaning and significance will last as long as *you* do? And what if they don't? What if a certain politician, or your employer, or your wealth, or your parents, a certain girl friend or boy friend, this or that possession, your health, or even your life don't last as long as you do?

And what we think of for ourselves, we also need to think of for our nation. When God decides to judge a proud nation, no economic expansion or improved job creation, no Stealth Bomber or Patriot Missiles, can save it. We make "the good" the enemy of "the best" if we mistake the means to an end for the end itself. Why have a nation militarily protected, economically prosperous, and politically sagacious, if the people's lives are not lived in humility and love for God and for others? However much social conditions encourage sin, conditions don't sin, people do. The nation which puts its trust finally and fully in its own strength is the nation which will feel the limits of that strength, and see the end of it, just as God promised to Edom here. If we learn any lesson about nations from the Bible, it is that God hates the arrogance of proud nations, and is committed to bringing them to realize the foolishness of trusting in anything other than Him. "'Though you soar like the eagle and make your nest among the stars, from there I will bring you down,' declares the LORD."

It's fashionable since Vietnam to write of American decline. Carl Henry's new book *Has Democracy Had Its Day?* presents disturbing facts of social breakdown in our country. They are no more disturbing, though, than they are true; we have to admit we have seen them. British decline has been an accepted fact of life for most of this century. The USSR has fallen, as did the short-lived empires of proud power built by Hitler and Mussolini, by Hirohito and Kaiser Wilhelm, by Franz Joseph of Austria, and we could go on and on, finding a decline for every rise of a great power in the history of the world. It appears that having power is in fact one of the most trying experiences which humans—individually or collectively—ever know.

When I had the privilege last year of opening the U. S. Senate in prayer for a couple of weeks, one theme I tried to bring into those prayers was that the permanency of these buildings must not deceive us. We must know that these buildings will one day crumble, and that the kingdom of God alone will remain. That does not for a moment give us a lack of appreciation for the buildings, or what goes on inside them. Rather, it gives us a correct perspective from which to view their significance.

Notice that Edom was proud without being anything like a superpower. It was a North Korea without nuclear weapons, an Iraq with no scuds. It was a small nation, but it was a proud nation. It was not that kind of healthy pride which causes people to take a certain amount of satisfaction in work well done, to try to care for and protect their family, and to understand what their own contribution can be. But the kind of pride which causes a nation to scorn the knowledge of God, to lay aside considerations of Him and His ways, of His laws, and His concern for justice.

This story, you see, shows us that God will judge not just proud peoples, but peoples whose overweening sense of self-importance leads them into defining their own rules for life, which leads them into doing things "their way, instead of God's way."

We see also that God will judge people for injustice. In verse 5, God turns to show that Edom's pride has led them into heinous sin; and He does this by comparing Edom's actions with those of robbers and grapegatherers. "If thieves came to you, if robbers in the night,... would they not steal only as much as they wanted? If grape pickers came to you, would they not leave a few grapes?"

In this verse, we have both a sign of Edom's injustice toward Israel, and of their correspondingly harsh judgment which God promises to them. Grape pickers would leave a gleaning at least; even thieves would take only what they needed, but you....

Anyone who has ever been the victim of a theft or robbery will know the strange thoughts of vulnerability, anger, the sense of having been in some sense violated by someone completely unknown to you. And yet, God says here to these people, even in that kind of experience everything hasn't been lost. Even that experience is inadequate to portray the injustice which the Edomites had committed. They had done something even worse.

The Edomites did not deserve, and therefore would not get even the kind of *partial* ruination which the Jews had received; the nations, says Obadiah, were going to enter the Edomite strongholds, and leave their towns empty and their houses bare. Verse 6 says, "How Esau will be ransacked, his hidden treasures pillaged!" This would be no ordinary defeat. It didn't matter how safe they thought their investments were, how well-protected their dwellings, all their protections and precautions would be completely useless, because in the person of the Babylonians the judgment of God was coming to conquer and to plunder. No protection would prove finally impenetrable. They would learn

God's Universal Standard

that with God's protection, there is safety even in the midst of unnumbered dangers, but without God's protection, all other protections are finally worthless.

And who better to be God's tools in all this than the very ones in whom the Edomites had trusted and relied and obeyed, instead of trusting and obeying and relying on God? Verse 7 notes, "Your allies will force you to the border; your friends will deceive and overpower you." The wise film director, you know, understands and exploits the gullible, inordinate trust which one character places in another who in reality is his mortal enemy. That's exactly the situation of the Edomites here in the way they regarded the Babylonians. But they would be betrayed. Their protectors were about to become their devourers. He says that "those who eat your bread will set a trap for you, but you will not detect it." They thought they were wise, beyond surprise; but the prophet says they were deceived. "You will not detect it."

The proud, God promises, will always be humbled. Those who practice injustice will always, in the end, suffer much more than those who are unjustly treated. The worst victims of atrocities have, without doubt, been the ones who held the guns, and thought themselves the victors.

And God would bring this crucial theological point home for all to see—that He loves justice, and abhors anyone less righteous, less loving, less merciful, less just than Himself, arrogating to themselves the right to treat other creatures as if they were *their's,* rather than God's.

But why was this befalling Edom now? What exactly had they done? How had their pride shown itself? In what particular injustice? That's what this next section is about, as we learn another bit of theology, that is, that God will judge people for opposing His people.

In verse 8 God restates His promise to bring Edom down, but in much more explicit terms this time. "'In that day,' declares the LORD, 'will I not destroy the wise men of Edom, men of understanding in the mountains of Esau?'" Perhaps God was being a bit sarcastic here, referring to these foolish people as wise; but even if not, it was clear that whatever cleverness and wits they had shown in their alliances was shallow and short-sighted. And whatever kind of wisdom it was, even this wisdom was not beyond the reach of God to destroy.

Neither their wise men nor their strong men could save them now. "Your warriors, O Teman, will be terrified, and everyone in Esau's mountains will be cut down in the slaughter." Why? "Because of the violence against your brother Jacob."

Christians in the Public Square

Now, I think this section may not strike us as it would have someone at another time, if for no other reason but for the anonymity with which we regard each other today. I dare say there are many who have witnessed suffering, not just on the television, but in person, and have done nothing to relieve it. Of course sometimes today that's entirely understandable, given the highly complex ways of dealing with things—police get involved, and ambulance teams, and doctors—we don't want to get in the way. But we need to remember that the ancient world wasn't like that.

Also, we need to rethink a bit about hospitality. Today, we tend to think of hospitality as a minor virtue—perhaps a kind greeting, or a generous offer of a meal. It's pleasant, but not a big deal, definitely optional. But it's interesting that throughout the Old Testament hospitality is presented as more important than that—some of the most important Old Testament stories are of hospitality being shown—Abraham, and his three angelic visitors, for example. In the Law, God's people were instructed to show hospitality. Punishments were clearly set out for those who did not show hospitality, and there was a most special responsibility to show hospitality to one's family. So hospitality is praised by Isaiah when he prophesies from the Lord saying that the kind of fast which pleases God is "to share your food with the hungry and to provide the poor wanderer with shelter—when you see the naked, to clothe him, and not to turn away from your own flesh and blood" (Isa. 58:7).

Now, you'll notice here in Obadiah that the tribes of the Edomites and the Israelites are referred to by the names of the individual ancestors to whom they traced their identity and their relationship. The Israelites were the descendants of Israel, that is, Jacob. And the Edomites were the descendants of Jacob's brother, Esau. So, here in verse 10, Israel is referred to as Edom's "brother Jacob."

This is mentioned here just to make more evident the outrage that Edom has committed. Not only has he not offered hospitality, but has instead committed violence, and that not just to a stranger, but to his own brother! Because of this outrage, God says, "you will be covered with shame." And not only will Edom be shamed before the nations, says the Lord, "you will be destroyed." And not destroyed in the sense of being temporarily exiled, like the people from Judah, but, he says, "destroyed forever."

In verse 11 Obadiah goes on to explain a bit more fully Edom's violence against Israel. Part of it was merely compliance with others who offered violence: "While strangers carried off his

God's Universal Standard

wealth and foreigners entered his gates and cast lots for Jerusalem," you stood aloof—"you were like one of them."

Anyone should have known better than to act as Edom did. And so God reproaches them in verse 12: "You should not look down on your brother in the day of his misfortune, nor rejoice over the people of Judah in the day of their destruction, nor boast so much in the day of their trouble." This word "look down" isn't just a passive staring. It has the sense of looking on, as if they were lying in wait anxiously, about to pounce, even, as some translations have it, gloating over what they saw. But they weren't just passive, were they? There was no even sham decency of averting their gaze; they joined in with their own brother's destroyers.

In verse 13: "You should not march through the gates of my people in the day of their disaster, nor look down on them in their calamity in the day of their disaster, nor seize their wealth in the day of their disaster." They gloated as though they had defeated someone else's brother, and now, like jackals, they would help exploit their weakness and plunder them. Edom became an accessory after the fact to the destruction, the murder, of his own brother.

If that seems too strong a representation of their crime, look at verse 14. "You should not wait at the crossroads to cut down their fugitives, nor hand over their survivors in the day of their trouble." God says, "At least thieves take only what they want; at least the grapegatherers leave a gleaning; but you waited at the crossroads to kill those who fled, and when you found survivors, you handed them over to their killers. Thieves are more considerate to their victims than you were to your own brother." The invaders may not have known the local roads, but these ancient collaborators knew exactly which way the trembling, miserable people of Judah would be fleeing, and it was in those very roads, reached perhaps after exhausting flight, grasping at their last thread of hope for survival, that the Edomites waited, waited in ambush, waited to ingratiate themselves to the powers that be by the blood of their victims. This was the tender mercy Edom showed his brother "in the day of his calamity." Like the wolf in the grandmother's bed in *Little Red Riding Hood,* where there should have been compassion, there was instead cruelty. Only this is no fairy tale. These injustices are every bit as real as any pictures you've seen from Bosnia on the television in the last year.

Considering this, the Edomites could hardly complain that *God* was being *too severe* on *them.* God will bring justice, He promises. Verse 15 says, "The day of the LORD is near for all nations." And if it's near for all nations, doesn't that include even, especially, the proud ones, the unjust ones, the oppressive ones like Edom?

In all of this disaster, we know from her own prophets that Judah had been punished by God in His sovereign rule of the nations. But that complexity of causation is beyond us. All we see is that the Babylonians and even Edom may have been God's means of judgment on Judah, but, at least according to this prophecy, the last thing Edom had in mind in all this was being God's minister. Just like the marauding hordes that wasted Job's family and wealth, who certainly never thought once of anything other than their own malicious desires, and yet were used by God as skillfully as the surgeon uses the cutting scalpel, so these Edomites were going to be used by God. But then the Babylonians would be used to bring God's judgment on the Edomites. "As you have done, it will be done to you; your deeds will return upon your own head." As Jesus said, "In the same way you judge others, you will be judged, and with the measure you use, it will be measured to you" (Matt. 7:2).

Verse 16 continues, "Just as you drank on my holy hill, so all the nations will drink continually; they will drink and drink and be as if they had never been."

Well, I think He is actually turning His attention there to Israel. He's saying that Israel has had the beginning of God's judgment, but from there it will go to all nations. As Peter wrote, "It is time for judgment to begin with the family of God, and if it begins with us, what will the outcome be for those who do not obey the gospel of God?" (1 Pet. 4:17). So, Obadiah is saying, even as judgment has begun with God's people, do you think that means you are going to get off any more lightly?

His people are an example, even as they prefigure Christ's role as the suffering servant. So God's judgment would continue on, as the cup of wrath is passed from Judah to Edom.

Now in all this situation, we naturally feel sympathy for people who are judged, because we are human. We understand what it is like to be "imperfect." We feel sympathetic toward the Israelites and outrage toward the Edomites.

But there is a special note of outrage in God's voice, as He presents those to whom *in particular* these Edomites were acting in such a prideful, arrogant, devouring way. Did you notice in verse 13 that God called the Israelites, "My people"? Injuries to anyone are affronts to a righteous God, but God especially protects the people He had marked out particularly as His own.

God's Universal Standard

It is always scandalous when we talk about God's concern for a particular people. But if you read the Bible, you can't get around the fact that God has always had a particular concern for those people to whom He has spoken, and who have accepted His word. Those to whom He has spoken and who have rejected His word are the focus of another kind of concern.

And this isn't just a theme of the Old Testament. Remember Jesus' words about the cities not receiving His disciples, "If anyone will not welcome you or listen to your words, shake the dust off your feet when you leave that home or town. I tell you the truth, it will be more bearable for Sodom and Gomorrah on the day of judgment than for that town" (Matt. 10:14-15). Or, as we read later, "God is just: He will pay back trouble to those who trouble you and give relief to you who are troubled, and to us as well. This will happen when the Lord Jesus is revealed from heaven in blazing fire with his powerful angels. He will punish those who do not know God and do not obey the gospel of our Lord Jesus" (2 Thess. 1:6-8). The biblical God, you see, is *not* an impersonal force, but a fiercely personal *lover*.

So, in this little book, we learn that God will judge the proud, the unjust, the opposers of His people, but we also see that God will take care of His people. Though their nation had fallen in judgment, God was not finished with the Israelites yet.

They too had suffered God's judgment, but their fate ultimately would be different from Edom's. In a just reversal of fortunes for Israel and Edom, we read in verse 17, "'But on Mount Zion will be deliverance; it will be holy, and the house of Jacob will possess its inheritance. The house of Jacob will be a fire and the house of Joseph a flame; the house of Esau will be stubble, and they will set it on fire and consume it. There will be no survivors from the house of Esau.' The LORD has spoken."

God here, in the midst of a word of judgment to Edom, speaks a word of hope to His people—that there would not only be justice for the wicked, but there would be restoration and revival for God's people. Here is hope in the midst of despair, as if they were going to be brought alive from the dead.

And so in the final verses, God promises His people that they will return from exile, and will regain their lost lands. And this is certainly final—finally to be fulfilled in the ultimate sense when God's people are in God's place under God's rule.

Look at the last phrase of this vision in verse 21: "The kingdom will be the LORD's." That's really the message throughout this little book.

But the question to us, to our churches, to our families and

Christians in the Public Square

our cities and our nation is, is this a word of encouragement or a warning. Certainly it was an encouragement to God's people. But remember this vision was addressed primarily, and unusually, to unbelievers. Why prophesy to unbelievers who were proud, unjust, and hardened? Because God wanted these people to know some theology. He wanted them to know that history—their lives, their actions—had meaning. He wanted them to know that God would one day draw a bottom line under all of history and pronounce the verdict—the true saying—about all the activities of humanity, against which there could be no appeal, no inadmissable evidence, no injustice, no hidden motives.

Some skeptics will certainly object, "Isn't the idea that history is going somewhere an illusion, invented to give our brief lives meaning?" Hitler watered the fields of Europe with the blood of millions—part of a thousand-year Reich. Marx' vision even today seeks to give peoples' lives meaning by putting them in the context of the inevitable march of history.

The political philosopher Karl Popper charges in his *magnum opus, The Open Society and its Enemies,* that any talk of meaning in history is to be feared, as preparing the grounds for tyranny, as the ends then can justify the means.

But, why are all of these people trying to find meaning in history? The fact that all these people have so grotesquely manipulated people's need for meaning, does that mean that there is no ultimate meaning in what we do with our lives?

Do you remember that great theological classic, *Raiders of the Lost Ark*? Where did they put the ark at the end of that movie? They put it in an ordinary-looking crate, in a warehouse with hundreds and thousands of crates that looked just like it. Sometimes, you see, counterfeits, instead of proving that there is nothing but counterfeits, suggest that there is an original–that there is a real meaning to history and life.

It's the nature of Christianity to bring a word, a promise from the future, by which we should direct our lives. So here we have God's word of warning for proud, unjust people who oppose Him. But we also have God's word of hope—He shall reign—for His people. So was Edom destroyed? Yes. In the next century, Edom was invaded from the south by Arabs, suffered wave after wave of invasions, and was essentially never reconstituted as a nation.

And were the Israelites restored? Yes, partially. But that fuller restoration is the restoration that the early Christian apostles talked about as Jews and non-Jews came together under the reign of God in their own lives, as they came to see that it is God who is to give their lives meaning.

God's Universal Standard

Jesus told the story in the New Testament of a man who was rich in things but who was ignorant of God, and just as he is in an expanding phase of his business, God speaks to Him in a dream, and calls him "Fool." "This night," he says, "your soul is required of you." "This is how it will be," says Jesus, "with anyone who stores up things for himself but is not rich toward God" (Luke 12:21).

There is nothing more practical, finally, for ourselves, for our businesses, our churches, our families, or our country, than *theology*.

TEN COMMANDMENTS FOR CHRISTIAN CITIZENS

By Charles G. Fuller

Several years ago, a highly publicized college basketball player was being interviewed by a sportscaster. Unfortunately, as is the case sometimes, the young man was obviously more basketball player than college student. As he talked about himself, the young man said, "You know, *I'm amphibious.* I can shoot with both hands!" Needless to say, this was one college student who had spent more time in the gym than in the dictionary!

Unlike the basketball player, many Christians today feel neither amphibious nor ambidextrous when it comes to the arenas of political and social debate. Some of us feel like fish out of water, tongue-tied, verbally ill-prepared, when it comes to practicing our faith in the public square. Other Christians have had a number overdone on them. They think we should stay out of the troubled waters of political and social issues, using our tongues solely to preach the gospel.

Certainly there is no debate about the primacy of our assignment while we live in this present world: Christians are to spread the gospel, love the lost, nurture the saved, with the goal of winning a world to Jesus! But there is something indisputably inherent about the gospel. By its very nature, the gospel is on a collision course with sin and evil, wherever sin and evil are found.

Christians in the Public Square

Living in a world where the Prince of Darkness wields such a heavy hand, it stands to reason the gospel will collide with more sin and evil in the public world than in the churchyard. At least we hope that's the case!

And another thing about the gospel—it is by its very nature transforming. So, as people are saved, their communities, their workplaces, the culture and society around them will sustain the impact of their transformation. Neither the gospel nor its accomplishments should be, nor can they be, hidden from view! What was it Jesus said? "Ye are the light of the world. A city that is set on an hill cannot be hid" (Matt. 5:14).

When God has citizens from His city to step onto any hill they cannot be hid, nor should they be, even if it's Capitol Hill!

I think two things are strange. First, it is strange to me that any group of Christians would think it justified to separate preaching the gospel from social ministries. And, second, I think it is strange any group of Christians would separate preaching the gospel from social issues.

How well I remember the 1960s and the great emphasis upon social ministries. In fact, the anti-institutional mentality of the 1960s so dominated the landscape, the traditional church and traditional church ministries were declared virtually passé. I remember reading and hearing, over and over, the claim that preaching as we had known it had had its day. There I was, fresh out of seminary, having taken Preaching 101 and 102, all dressed up with no place to go!

What I most remember about those days was hearing some say we should minister to people's needs, in the name of Christ, with no ulterior motive to lead them to Christ. That baffled me. How could it be virtuous to feed, clothe, shelter, protect, and care for people while withholding from them the very best thing you had to offer?

I am no less baffled, thirty years later, by the idea some espouse that we should preach a gospel of personal conversion which can have impact on selected social issues, but avoid those issues which have political ownership and volatility. To be sure, it is neither wise nor necessary to die on every hill of every pet peeve our fellow Christians may have, but if it is a subject of biblical morality and justice, how dare we muzzle God's voice on the issue?

Baptists are rightfully strong on the matter of separation of church and state. I come from a part of the country, Virginia, that knows something about the prices paid in other days for that territory of American freedom. And we ought to hold our own feet to the fire on that issue when we are tempted to use the

Ten Commandments for Christian Citizens

government to evangelize and Christianize America! That is *our* job! But we also ought to hold the government's feet to the fire when it oversteps its bounds and restricts our civil liberty to declare openly our faith and the opinions of our faith about moral issues! All I ask from government is the provision and protection of the level ground of free expression.

I remain mystified as to why profanity, vulgarity, and the products of depraved entertainment fall under the category of protected speech, but public prayer and voluntary religious remarks by students do not.

We are told by some we need no religious liberty amendment to the Constitution, for the First Amendment is thoroughly adequate to guarantee our freedom of religion. To be sure, the First Amendment does not need to be rewritten, but when a thirty-year zeal has been invested in applying the Establishment Clause of the amendment to the neglect of the Free Exercise Clause, there is a need for an interpretive course correction. Otherwise, the ground gets less and less level under the feet of the folks who look to me to be very much like the people who founded this country.

And while we are on the subject of checks and balances, I believe we Southern Baptists need to keep our own courses under scrutiny. Whether it be national politics, or denominational politics, we should never take a moral stance on the basis of its popularity in the group with which we want to be identified. If it's right, it's biblically right. If it's wrong, it's biblically wrong. Moral issues for God's people are not political credentials and passkeys; they are moral issues!

Others may differ, but as for me, the pulpit behind which I stand will not fail to address matters God's Word addresses, but I will not hitch that pulpit to a political candidate's star. In my view, that is a demotion for the pulpit! There are numerous politicians who are my kind of Americans, and I will vote for them, but they are not always my kind of Christians. The gospel is never to be sold out or sold short, so it should not be compromised by identifying it with someone who may represent the best of your politics but not the best of your witness.

Make no question of it, Christians have a rightful place in the public square, but it is a place which is no less distinctively Christian than when we take our places in the pew, the loft, or the pulpit.

Peter's first epistle was written to first-century Christians who knew a lot more about anti-Christian bias than we. To those believers who lived in hostile surroundings, Peter offered both words of comfort and words of instruction.

Christians in the Public Square

Dearly beloved, I beseech you as strangers and pilgrims, abstain from fleshly lusts, which war against the soul; having your conversation honest among Gentiles: that, whereas they speak against you as evildoers, they may by your good works, which they shall behold, glorify God in the day of visitation. Submit yourselves to every ordinance of man for the Lord's sake: whether it be to the king, as supreme; or unto governors, as unto them that are sent by him for the punishment of evildoers, and for the praise of them that do well. For so is the will of God, that with well doing ye may put to silence the ignorance of foolish men: as free, and not using your liberty for a cloak of maliciousness, but as the servants of God (1 Pet. 2:11-16).

It would appear the 17th verse is a clear statement of four commandments for Christian citizens living in a world where the public square was not nearly so available as ours: "Honour all men. Love the brotherhood. Fear God. Honour the king."

In the spirit of that set of instructions, I would like to offer ten commandments for Christian citizens living in America on the threshold of the twenty-first century, and who do have access to the public square.

1. *Honor Your Citizenship.*

You and I do not *deserve* to be Americans, we are *privileged* to be Americans. We have the right to see our faults, monitor our failures, speak our piece, debate our point, grumble if we choose, challenge the positions of elected officials, be angered by moral erosion, but it is not our right to *dishonor* our country.

It is to the extent we cherish our privileges and exercise our role in preserving national rudiments that we are responsible citizens. To love America is to honor all that is good about her, while seeking to protect her from all that would destroy her goodness.

2. *Know Your Heritage.*

Among the world's nations, the United States of America may be young, but our heritage is no less rich or distinctive. Unless we are watchful, however, there are those who will methodically make a totally secular country of us despite the great Judeo-Christian foundation underlying the birth of this nation. The revisionists, with their humanist-secular agenda, should be constantly impeded and challenged by those who know, and know they know, the American story.

Ten Commandments for Christian Citizens

3. *Live Your Values.*

It is one thing to extol high moral values and to be hard on those who seek to lower them. It is another thing to prove your morality in the body and behavior of your own flesh!

Having your conversation honest among the Gentiles: that, whereas they speak against you as evildoers, they may by your good works, which they shall behold, glorify God in the day of visitation (1 Pet. 2:12).

4. *Maintain Your Prayer Life.*

If you believe as I, in the Divine inspiration of the *entire* Word of God, you must give as much reverence to 1 Timothy 2 as to John 3. We are to pray for government officials. I believe we are to pray for their salvation. We are to pray for their wisdom, teachability, and sense of accountability. And for those with whom we disagree, we are to pray, avoiding a hostile and punitive spirit. Above all, we are to pray for God's intervention and protection from human error in matters of the nation's life and destiny.

5. *Voice Your Convictions.*

We are to do so through every legitimate channel given us, with a courteous forthrightness. "For so is the will of God, that with well doing ye may put to silence the ignorance of foolish men" (1 Pet. 2:15).

6. *Discipline Your Criticisms.*

Not everything about America is wrong. Not everything which takes place in Congress, in the State House, or in City Council is in need of our protest. Public officials and wholesome legislation, as well as positive influences, need to be commended and encouraged by Christian citizens.

7. *Analyze Your Zeal.*

Needless to say, we cannot give equal time and effort to every noble crusade in which Christians can be involved. Hence, a certain amount of selectivity must be exercised. We must be honest, however, about what motivates that selectivity. God forbid we would ever be selectively moral!

For us to be strong and vocal in our opposition to abortion, the homosexual agenda, pornography, and the gambling lobby, while apparently suffering from lockjaw on matters of racial injustice, may reveal we are more motivated by personal appeal than by moral consistency!

I want to commend the Christian Life Commission and others for leading Southern Baptists at the 1995 meeting of the Southern Baptist Convention in Atlanta to adopt the statement

Christians in the Public Square

acknowledging our past failures in matters of racial equality. And to the few who questioned the validity of apologizing for the failures of previous generations, let me remind you that though we are not guilty of Adam's sin, we surely have to acknowledge his guilt and the ongoing impact of it!

8. *Protect Your Family.*

There can be little question that at the bull's eye of Satan's strategy to take America is our home and family life. Again we must stand against the revisionists who seek to redefine the family to suit the corruptions they dare to call family values for an enlightened America.

9. *Extend Your Compassion.*

Too often we assume our sole task in resisting social and moral evil is to publicly condemn it! If we expect to be heard when we say our Lord hates the sin but loves the sinner, we will have to be living proof texts with hands-on ministries to those victimized by their own sin.

10. *Declare Your Hope.*

In all our strivings for that which is right for America, we must not place the hope of it all in the lap of human response. As vital as our efforts may be, as important as election outcomes may be, as crucial as the debates over moral issues may be, the hope of America lies squarely in the hands of a sovereign God, the Judge of earth, who will always do right! His side wins!

> Careless seems the great Avenger;
>   history's pages but record,
> One deathgrapple in the darkness
>   'twixt old systems and the Word;
> Truth forever on the scaffold,
>   Wrong forever on the throne,
> Yet that scaffold sways the future,
>   and, behind the dim unknown,
> Standeth God within the shadow,
>   keeping watch above his own.[1]

In God we *must* trust!

Endnotes

[1] James Russell Lowell, "The Present Crisis," *Masterpieces of Religious Verse* (New York: Harper & Brothers Publishers, 1948), 523.

AMERICA: AN ECOTONIC MOMENT IN TIME

By O. S. Hawkins

America is presently in the midst of an ecotonic moment in time. An "ecotone" is a technological word from the world of biology that describes a particular place where two ecosystems merge and blend together. I first heard of the word while living in the city of Fort Lauderdale, Florida. There is a particular place where the intercoastal waterway and the new river come together that forms an ecotone. The salt water from the Atlantic Ocean flows into Port Everglades and into the intercoastal waterway. From the Everglades just west of Fort Lauderdale, the fresh water flows through the new river, making its way toward the ocean. At the particular place where this salt water and fresh water blend and merge together, an ecotone develops. Ecotones are places of tremendous possibility. Often fish lay their eggs there. Ecotones can also be very problematic to those who are engaged in the battles of ecology.

At this point in time we are experiencing an ecotonic stage in American life. Two worlds are blending and merging together at the same time. One is a modern world and the other a post-modern world. The world in which many of us in the baby-boomer generation were educated is history. All the cumulative knowledge of world history will double within the next five years. Our world is transforming at breakneck speed into a post-modern era. This

Christians in the Public Square

presents a time of tremendous possibility for those of us who can translate the message of our Christian heritage to a world that is in desperate need without changing the heart of its message. It is also a time of tremendous problems for those who are seeking to translate the gospel to our world in the same way we did ten, twenty, or thirty years ago. The western world is not so much in debate over whether the Bible is true as it is in whether it is relevant. That is, does this Book written in an ancient Middle Eastern culture have any relevancy in a world where we are transplanting organs, going to the moon, and experimenting with genetic engineering? They will never know unless we deal with some of the major questions of our day.

We are living and ministering in a day when the church's influence is waning in a secular society. We are seeing the product of an entire generation that has been reared with virtually no moral absolutes in the home, in many of their schools, and tragically in many of their churches. This past Sunday Great Britain saw less than five percent of its population in any kind of house of worship. History records that civilizations which see the collapse of the home and accompanying moral values do not last past one or two generations unless a spiritual awakening occurs. In America we are watching the disintegration of a culture in our own lifetime. We have lost the concept of personal responsibility for our own transgressions, and all of our maladies have become someone else's fault.

Recently I walked through the Vietnam memorial in our nation's capital. I saw etched in the granite wall name after name of young people who left their homes and never came back. Some of those names were more than just letters etched in granite; they were personal friends from my high school days. As I looked at that wall, I realized they would be in their middle forties today. If by some miracle they could step out of that wall and go back to their hometowns, they would see a world that is totally different from the one they knew. They would wonder why we have become a nation where more than half of our marriages end in divorce. As they walked the streets of their small towns and cities, they would wonder why the Judeo-Christian ethic was but a memory. As they revisited their schoolhouses, they would be shocked to learn that it is now illegal for children to pray in the same classrooms where they were educated. They would be floored to realize that the Gideons could no longer hand them a New Testament on the campuses of their schools, but organizations such as Planned Parenthood are often free to dispense condoms at no charge. They would be surprised to discover that in many of their small towns

America: An Ecotonic Moment in Time

the traditional manger scene was no longer on the courthouse lawn. They would be shocked to see that homosexual lifestyles were legitimized and promoted by much of the rhetoric, appointments, and actions of those who live in the White House. As they visited their schools, they would be shocked to pass through metal detectors and see that teenage pregnancy was rampant. Those who lost their lives at such a young age would be appalled to hear that we legally kill 1.5 million babies a year in America today through abortion. As they strolled past the vacant lots and playgrounds of their neighborhoods, they would be shocked at the way they are terrorized by gangs and drive-by shootings. As they looked around, they would wonder what happened to the godly male leadership which has disappeared from so many of the homes of America.

We should make no mistake about it. The United States is morally bankrupt in large part because we have been led by a liberal philosophy that has made false assumptions about two particular things: the nature of the universe, and the nature of mankind. Liberal philosophy seldom asks "why?" It only asks "what?" One can take almost any issue. Take the issue of drugs. Few in the liberal establishment are asking "why?" Most of them only ask "what?" What can we do about this problem? So we dispense free needles to try to clean up the process. This particular point is seen daily with the issue of the HIV virus and the accompanying AIDS epidemic. Not enough people in Washington are asking "why?" It does not seem to be politically correct. So we only ask "what?" What can we do about the AIDS epidemic? And the answers we are given are more education, how to have safe sex, and the like. We are asking "what?" when we ought to be asking "why?" about these major moral issues of life. Have you ever thought about why we are called "conservatives"? We are trying to conserve something. We are trying to conserve some traditional moral values that have made America what it has been in the past. These values were conserved by people asking "why" and not "what. "

The prophet of old, Jeremiah, lived and ministered in a day much like ours. The nation of Judah had been blessed. They had prospered, but they forgot their roots. They forgot their God. They began to think they were indestructible, and the final result came in 586 B.C. when they were defeated by Nebuchadnezzar and taken away into Babylonian captivity. Jeremiah was a man who lived with a burden for the way in which his country had turned its back on God. He had seen the blessing. Now he observed the collapse and corruption from within. With a weeping heart he asks, "Where

Christians in the Public Square

is the Lord that brought us up out of the land of Egypt" (Jer. 2:6)? Then he came straight to the bottom line by quoting the Lord Himself regarding His people, "They have turned their back unto me, and not their face" (Jer. 2:27). As I read these words in this Book of all books, I cannot help but see our own America. I believe God is asking today, "Where is the Lord Who brought you out of Egypt?" I believe He is asking us, "Why have you turned your back to me and not your face?"

Jeremiah asks four hard questions in chapter 8 of the book that bears his name. Interestingly enough, unlike the liberalism of our day, he did not ask "what?" Jeremiah asked "why?" These are the four "whys" America needs to be asking herself today. "Why is this people...slidden back?" (Jer. 8:5). "Why do we sit still?" (Jer. 8:14). "Why have they provoked [God] to anger?" (Jer. 8:19). "Why is not the health...recovered?" (Jer. 8:22). Is there a recovery for the western world?

What would happen if the President of the United States would stand up before the American people and stop asking "what?" and begin to seriously probe and ask "why?" Why have we slidden back? Why do we sit still? Why have we provoked a holy God to anger? Why does there seem to be no recovery? Let's ask ourselves these questions of Jeremiah's day today:

Why Has This People Slidden Back?

Why then is this people of Jerusalem slidden back by a perpetual blacksliding? They hold fast deceit, they refuse to return (Jer. 8:5).

Jeremiah says the people of his nation held fast to deceit and refused to return. That is, they and we continue to believe a lie. America today seems to be without a knowledge of spiritual things. We hold fast to deceit and refuse to return. On February 4, 1995, our *Dallas Morning News* carried a guest column by then Mayor Steve Bartlett. He said, "Up until thirty years ago, strong moral values were a part of our daily lives and experiences. They were a part of everything that we did. But in the course of those thirty years we've walked away from those values and put them in a closet. I don't know *why* [emphasis mine] that happened. I only know that it happened."

Thirty years ago? Mr. Mayor, you are right. Let us remember what happened thirty years ago. For one thing the Supreme Court struck down school prayer by prohibiting this simple invocation, "Almighty God we acknowledge our dependency upon you and beg your blessings on us, our parents, our teachers, and our country." That was it! No mention of the Lord Jesus Christ. It was just a

America: An Ecotonic Moment in Time

simple petition asking God to bless four things: the students, the parents, the teachers, and the country.[1] It is shocking to examine what has happened to those four entities over the last thirty years.

The invocation struck down by the Supreme Court called for God's blessings upon "us" (that is, the students.) What has happened to the American student in the past thirty years? We have the highest rate of teen motherhood in the western world. Each year one million teenage girls become pregnant. In our own city of Dallas some schools are equipped with as many as fifteen nursery beds to take care of the babies that are born from teen mothers who are still in school. Should we be surprised when we have asked "what" instead of "why" throughout these years? We ask "what" can we do about the dilemmas, and so we decided to hand out condoms and forbid groups like Gideons to pass out New Testaments.

The petition asked the blessing of God upon our "parents." What has happened to the parenthood in America in the last thirty years? We lead the world in divorce. One and one-half million children run away from home every year. Sex abuse seems to be rampant, and the home is disintegrating. But the liberal establishment is only asking "what?"

The third part of the petition was the invocation of a blessing upon our "teachers." What has happened to the American education system in the last thirty years? In *Stone vs. Gramm* in 1980 the court decided, "If posted copies of the Ten Commandments are to have any effect at all, it would be to induce children to meditate upon them and perhaps obey, and this is not permissible. The First Amendment protects it." God forbid that a child obey one of the Ten Commandments. And the result for teachers? School violence, metal detectors, and plummeting SAT scores.

The final request was a blessing of God upon our "country." What has happened to the United States of America in the last thirty years? Violent crime is up five hundred times over what it was in those days. It is no longer safe to walk on many of the streets of the cities and towns of America. And, here we are asking "what?" The real question is "why?" Why has this occurred? Because so many good people have done nothing.

Jeremiah goes on to say that "my people know not the judgment of the LORD" (Jer. 8:7). It seems as though he is speaking of America and not Judah. The judgment of God is seldom heard in any of the pulpits of America any longer. Speak of the judgment of God in the city of Washington, D.C., and you'll be scoffed and laughed out of town by the social and liberal elite. But God has not

Christians in the Public Square

abdicated His throne. He is still in control. As Daniel says, "He still rules over the affairs of men." Ask Israel if this is true. Ask Judah if this is true. Ask Rome or the former Union of Soviet Socialist Republics. Jeremiah says that even migratory birds know when it is time to return home (Jer. 8:7). But Judah did not, nor does America. We have less wisdom than a bird.

Jeremiah continues as though he were speaking to the issues of our own day. Hear him ask, "How do you say, 'We are wise and the law of the LORD is with us?'...They have rejected the word of the LORD; and what wisdom is in them?" (Jer. 8:8-9). Is anything more applicable to the United States of America than these words? We have rejected the Word of God for the wisdom of man's own liberal agenda, and we wonder why as the question comes in Verse 5, "Why has this people slidden back?" He goes on quoting the Lord Himself, "I will give their wives unto others" (Jer. 8:10). Does this sound like America, where more than half the marriages end in divorce? Is the judgment of God upon this nation? Jeremiah speaks of those who say, "Peace, peace; when there is no peace" (Jer. 8:11). Those in the White House and many in the halls of Congress put their spin doctors on every issue saying, "Peace, peace," when there is no peace.

False prophets in Judah such as those in America only deal superficially with societal ills. This was never more exemplified than in the recent United Nations Fourth World Conference on Women in Bejing, China, in 1995. What did the President of the United States say regarding this conference? He said, "However anyone might try to paint this conference, the truth is it is true blue to families—to supporting them, to conserving them, to valuing them.[2] Listen to some of the topics of this particular conference. There were seminars on "lesbianism for the curious," "lesbian activism from an interfaith perspective," "lesbianism in motherhood: talking about being sperm donors," "lesbian flirtation techniques workshop,"[3] and on and on. Bella Abzug on the second day of the conference joined hands with other women in a prayerful tribute to "mother earth" that virtually mocked orthodox Christian belief. They prayed, "Thanks to mother earth, for you give life...no more crucifixion...we celebrate the life not the crucifixion...we are power!" Then, thrusting their hands in the air, they began to shout, "I am power, I am power, I am power."[4] That sounds strangely like an experience in Genesis 11 that lives on in infamy known as the Tower of Babel.

And what was the position of the leader of the free world? He said this conference was true blue to families. And we wonder, "Why is this people slidden back?" We have leadership that

America: An Ecotonic Moment in Time

continues to say, "Peace, peace," when there is no peace.

Jeremiah speaks to his people and so poignantly to us about the greatest tragedy of all when he says, "Were they ashamed when they had committed abomination? Nay, they were not at all ashamed, neither could they blush" (Jer. 8:12). This is our greatest tragedy. There seems to be no shame. There is a blatant disregard in America for anything that is moral or pure. On inauguration day our President began the day by putting his hand on the Bible, which was open to Galations 6:9-10 which says, "Let us not be weary in well doing: for in due season we shall reap, if we faint not." He ended the day by dropping his daughter off at the MTV ball and joining his friends at the gay ball. It is too bad he didn't read the two verses immediately in front of the ones he had chosen. Galations 6:7-8 says, "Be not deceived; God is not mocked: for whatsoever a man soweth, that shall he also reap. For he that soweth to his flesh shall of the flesh reap corruption; but he that soweth to the Spirit shall of the Spirit reap life everlasting."

We should not blame the politicians for the moral collapse of America. We need to put it where it belongs, at the feet of the church. Biblical moral standards are forgotten in an attempt to appease an immoral culture, and in some ways to "market" the church to a secular world.

It would be well to remember that the context of Jeremiah 8 is found in 2 Chronicles 34. In that particular chapter good King Josiah had begun to ask some whys instead of whats. His trusted friend, Hilkiah, had discovered the Word of God, which had been lost in the house of God. He brought it to the king, and a tremendous turning to God ensued. This is our greatest need, that the church would find this Book, and take it to the king. The king led that nation to take a stand on the Word of God, and the country began to prosper once again.

We wonder why, in the words of Jeremiah, we are "slidden back." The answer is in the fact that the salt has lost its savor. Some time ago I received a form letter from the head of Americans United for the Separation of Church and State in which he was bemoaning the fact that some Christian ministers in America were trying to, in his words, "Christianize America." I am unapologetically trying to Christianize America, and the entire world, for that matter! This is the commission our Lord gave us before He left.

One of my pastoral predecessors at the First Baptist Church in Dallas, the late and great Dr. George W. Truett, stood on the Capitol steps of our nation on May 16, 1920, and gave one of the greatest messages on religious liberty ever heard. In the course of

Christians in the Public Square

his message, he said, "The one transcending and inspiring influence in victory is the Christian faith. Civilization without Christianity is doomed. Let there be no hesitation nor apology for the insistence that the one hope for the individual, the one hope for society, for civilization, is the Christian religion." That doesn't sound like toleration or pluralism to me.

Why is this people slidden back? That's a good question. Jeremiah goes on to quote the Lord Himself. "The things that I have given them shall pass away from them" (Jer. 8:13). If God said this of Judah, the apple of His eye, why do you think He wouldn't say the same of any other nation? If America does not start dealing with the whys instead of the whats, judgment is coming. America no longer believes that God controls the created order. We may give Him the occasional tip of a hat at a prayer breakfast or the like, but He, by and large, has no place in the affairs of men, particularly, in the places of power. The question is not "what?" The question is "why?" Jeremiah continues with another "why?":

Why Do We Sit Still?

Why do we sit still? Assemble yourselves, and let us enter into the defenced cities, and let us be silent there: for the LORD our God hath put us to silence, and given us water of gall to drink, because we have sinned against the LORD (Jer. 8:14).

Many Americans have bought into the liberal lies, media manipulation, and public propaganda. The tragedy is the church sits by with a false confidence based on lying words, saying, "Peace, peace, when there is no peace." We need to ask ourselves the question, "Why do we sit still?" It has not always been the case. Don't listen to those who say that religious principles played little part in the founding of the United States of America. Don't listen to those who say that we were basically not built on a Judeo-Christian philosophy but on more of a pluralistic deistic philosophy. Forever etched in the charters of the original thirteen colonies is the gospel truth. Rhode Island was established in 1683, and in their charter they said, "We submit ourselves, our lives, our estates unto the Lord Jesus Christ, the King of Kings, and the Lord of Lords, and to all those perfect and most absolute laws given in His Holy Word." Maryland's charter says it was "formed by a pious zeal to extend the Christian gospel." Delaware was "formed for the further propagation of the holy gospel." When the founders of Connecticut wrote their charter, they said that Connecticut was there to "preserve the purity of the gospel of the

America: An Ecotonic Moment in Time

Lord Jesus Christ." It certainly doesn't sound like Connecticut was too pluralistic in its beginnings. There's talk of Washington, D.C., becoming the fifty-first state. Can you imagine what their charter might read?

Note the following quote and see if you can identify the author.

> I believe no one can read the history of our country without realizing the good Book and the Spirit of the Saviour have from the beginning been our guiding genius. We are a Christian land, governed by Christian principles. I believe the entire Bill of Rights came into being because of the knowledge our forefathers had in the Bible and their belief in it. I believe we are living today in the spirit of the Christian religion. I like to also believe that, as long as we do, no great harm will come to this country.

Who said that? Jerry Falwell? Pat Robertson? Pat Buchanan? Those were the words of Chief Justice Earl Warren on February 15, 1954. He is remembered today as a social liberal. Can you imagine a Bill Clinton appointee saying anything like that today? In one brief generation we have moved from asking the why questions to the what questions, and the tragedy is that the church has simply "sat still."

Jeremiah's question comes thundering down through the corridors of the centuries to us today: "Why do we sit still?" America's biggest problem is an apathetic church who has lost her first love. And in losing that first love, we have also lost our influence. We have simply sat still for a generation. When I see political leaders with their liberal agendas contrary to the Word of God coming out of church on Sunday being photographed with Bibles in their hands and waving to the television cameras, the words of Jeremiah 7:9 10 ccho in my mind: "Will ye steal, murder, commit adultery, and swear falsely, and burn incense unto Baal, and walk after other gods whom ye know not, and come and stand before me in this house, which is called by my name, and say, 'We are delivered to do all these abominations'?" In the midst of a changing ecotonic world that can go either way, we must stop asking "what" and begin to ask "why." Why are we slidden back? Why do we sit still? Jeremiah continues with another question:

Why Have They Provoked Me to Anger?

Behold the voice of the cry of the daughter of my people ...in a far country: 'Is not the LORD in Zion? Is not her king in her?' 'Why have they provoked me to anger with

Christians in the Public Square

their graven images, and with strange vanities?' (Jer. 8:19).

God asks us another question through Jeremiah's prayer: "Why have they provoked me to anger with their carved images—with foreign idols?" America did not abandon God. We just made Him one of many others. New-age humanistic thought which exalts man over Christ has taken center stage. It is no wonder those with liberal agendas do not want the Ten Commandments in the classroom. The very first one says, "You shall have no other gods before me." He is a jealous God. We have supported a pluralism which tolerates a form of Christianity that does not make any demands on a culture. It is a form of Christianity that only asks what and never asks why. Christianity is not just another person's opinion. It is objective truth. We have provoked a Holy God to anger in that we have allowed other gods to share His glory.

How did the early Christians engage their culture? What was it about them that caused the Roman Empire to put them to death in the Coliseum and other places of public exploitation and execution? Why the Christians when other conquered peoples of the world did not meet the same fate? The answer is found in one of the ruins of Rome. It is called the Pantheon, the temple of all gods. Some time ago, while returning from a trip to Africa, I took my family to visit this impressive edifice. As you walk into the temple, you find around all of the walls niches carved in the stone. When the Romans would conquer a certain people who, for example, might worship the god Jupiter, they would bring them to the Pantheon and say, "Here is a niche for Jupiter. You can worship him anytime you desire." They appeased their conquered peoples in such a fashion. Perhaps they conquered a people who worshiped the god Juno. They would bring them there to the Pantheon and give them a niche for Juno. When they brought the Christians back to Rome in the triumph of their military conquest, they took them also to the Pantheon. In effect, they said, "We are going to give you a niche for Jesus here between Jupiter and Juno." The Christians said, "No! There is only one Lord"—and they gave their lives for that.

Agnostic, apathetic America has no sense that we have provoked a holy God to anger. In fact, we scoff at the idea. He says, "Do not commit murder." And we kill 1.5 million babies a year. He says, "Do not commit adultery." And we live in a sex-crazed society. When Paul wrote the Roman letter, he foresaw Rome's coming collapse, and in chapter 1 spoke of a culture that had been given over to depraved minds.

America: An Ecotonic Moment in Time

America is agnostic toward spiritual things. We have an "in your face" attitude toward a holy God. There is no real sense in the executive, legislative, or judicial branches of government that we are provoking a holy God to anger. So we continue on our way asking "what?" when we ought to be asking "why?" Why have we slidden back? Why do we sit still? Why have we provoked God to anger? Jeremiah asks the final why:

Why Is There No Recovery?

Is there no balm in Gilead; is there no physician there? Why then is not the health of the daughter of my people recovered?" (Jer. 8:22).

Is there any answer? Is it too late? People in Jeremiah's day did not repent, and there was no recovery. They were taken into Babylonian captivity and hung their harps on the willow trees of Babylon because they could not sing the Lord's song in a foreign land. Jeremiah asks, "Is there no balm in Gilead; is there no physician there? Why then is not the health of the daughter of my people recovered?" (Jer. 8:22). Yes, there is indeed a health-care crisis in America today, but it is not primarily physical nor mental. It is a spiritual health-care crisis.

Is it too late for us as it was for Judah? Where is the answer? Is there no balm in Gilead? Is there no physician here? Yes, there is a Great Physician. If you go to your personal physician with a physical need, he examines you and gives you a prescription. God gives us a prescription in Jeremiah 3:22: "Return, ye backsliding children, and I will heal your blackslidings." Yes, thank God, there is still a Physician. The return begins with you and me. Not the politicians. Not the school systems. But with the church of Jesus Christ.

We are living in what has become more and more of a pagan culture, not unlike the one with which the early church was confronted. In fact, they were under a tremendous amount of persecution we have really not seen in America as of yet. For example, in Acts 12 the leader of the church in Jerusalem, Simon Peter, was incarcerated by the authorities for his moral stands and for the gospel's sake. Acts 12:5 says, "Peter was kept in prison, but prayer was made without ceasing of the church unto God for him." The church of Jesus Christ has forgotten our primary battlefield. It is very difficult to win a war if you do not know where the battle is being fought. Some of us have forgotten this. That is, while Peter was kept in prison, the church was praying earnestly for him. If Acts 12:5 had been written about the twentieth-century church, it might read, "Peter was kept in prison, but the church

Christians in the Public Square

picketed City Hall on his behalf." It might read, "Peter was kept in prison, but the church protested with a mass campaign on his behalf." It might read, "Peter was kept in prison, but the church took over the local precincts in order to make some changes in the elected officials." It might say, "Peter was kept in prison, but the church signed petitions on his behalf."

This early church engaged their culture. How? They had the power of God upon them. They knew where the battle was being fought. Go to Ephesus today and walk through the ancient ruins of that first-century metropolis. It amazed me as I did so. As I walked through the amphitheater, down the streets, into the bathhouses and the libraries and the temples of that ancient world, I wondered, how was that city captured for Christ? Paul went there with just a couple of friends and engaged the culture and saw the transformation of a whole city. How? There was no explanation for it but the power of God—the power of God in response to a praying church. If some of us who are called by the name of the Lord would spend as much time listening to God as we do certain talk-show hosts on the radio or television, we would be on our way to revival. Some of us do not think we need God because we have a conservative political agenda to follow.

Is there a recovery? Yes, the most important thing we can do is call upon the name of the Lord in prayer, and then begin to ask some whys and elect some leaders with character and genuine moral backbone. It was not the Babylonians who brought Judah low. God only used them. It was God Himself who did it. Why? The answer is in 2 Chronicles 28:19: "The Lord brought Judah low because of Ahaz king of Israel; for he made Judah naked, and transgressed sore against the LORD."

What did God do? God Himself brought the nation of Judah low. We can blame it on economics, budget deficits, the welfare system, the collapse of moral values, but God still rules in the affairs of men. There is someone in Washington not being factored into the equation. Our leadership is blind to the fact that "the most High ruleth in the kingdom of men" (Dan. 4:32). Could it be that behind all the politics is God Himself allowing all of this to happen in America?

And what did God do to Judah? He brought them low. Why? Because their leader, their king, had encouraged a moral decline in the land. Ahaz was personally immoral and unfaithful, and his policies reflected his own character. It is one thing to be immoral, but another to "encourage a moral decline in the land." We have had presidents of the United States in the past who have been known for immoral acts. But it is quite another thing to encourage

America: An Ecotonic Moment in Time

immorality through people and policies. A leader encourages a moral decline in the land when he takes a pen in hand and signs an executive order permitting the bodies of aborted babies to be used in research. A leader encourages a moral decline in the land when he appoints an AIDS czar who quickly says that America is a "repressed Victorian society" and tells the populous, including teenagers, to seek pleasure in sex. A leader encourages a moral decline in the land when he favors the distribution of condoms in the public school systems of America. A leader encourages a moral decline in the land when he only asks "what" and seldom ever asks "why." A leader encourages a moral decline in the land when he appoints twenty-six openly and publicly professing homosexuals to executive branch positions. And we should not simply be talking about Democratic leadership. There is a lot of Republican leadership that has no moral fiber in our nation as well.

Leaders of nations bear moral responsibilities, and we do ourselves a tremendous injustice if we do not elect godly men and women to leadership.

There is a remedy for us. It is the only remedy, and it is not found in the ballot box or on television ads or in curriculum. The remedy is found at the foot of a Roman cross outside the city walls of Jerusalem where the conquering Christ was "made sin for us that we might become the righteousness of God in Him."

We are living in the most important days of American history. It is indeed an ecotonic moment in our nation's history. Two worlds are blending and merging together. It is a time of tremendous possibility. It is not too late if we stop asking "what?" and begin to ask "why?" Why are we slidden back? We have forgotten our roots. Why do we sit still? Because an apathetic church has forgotten where the battle is being fought. Why have we provoked a holy God to anger? Because we have shared His glory with other gods around us. And, why is there no remedy? Is there no balm in Gilead? Is there no physician there? Yes, the Great Physician is still ready and willing to bless our nation as He did in the beginning. Jeremiah said it best when he said, "Ask for the old paths, where is the good way, and walk therein, and ye shall find rest for your souls" (Jer. 6:16). What is America's greatest need? Don't blame politicians for the moral collapse. Don't point the finger at the education system. All these are simply fruits of a root problem. We have a generation in America that does not know Christ primarily because the church has not made Him known. What is our greatest need? It is found in 2 Chronicles 34. The Church of Jesus Christ needs to find the Book of God in the house of God and take it to the king!

Christians in the Public Square

Endnotes

[1] David Barton, *America: To Pray or Not to Pray* (Aledo, Texas: Wallbuilder Press, 1988), 11.

[2] "Transcript of Aug. 26 Remarks by President, First Lady on 75th Anniversary of Ratification of 19th Amendment," U.S. Newswire, Aug. 28, 1995.

[3] Schedule of Activities, NGO Forum on Women—Beijing '95, Aug. 30-Sept. 8, 1995, 35, 41, 49, 58, 98, 103, 110, 133, 134, 190, 195, 198.

[4] George Archibald, "Forum Fights Over Free Sex; Anti-Vatican Group Says Bible Backs It," *The Washington Times*, Sept. 1, 1995, A1.

BEING SALT AND LIGHT IN AMERICA

By Gary Bauer

My oldest daughter, a few months back, left to go to her freshman year in college at William and Mary in Virginia. In the summer, leading up to her leaving home, she spent a lot of time rereading the old classics that she thought she would have to be familiar with in college. One of them was *A Tale of Two Cities* by Charles Dickens. We remember the famous first line of that book: "It was the best of times and it was the worst of times." I found myself thinking that even though that line was written about England and France many years ago, it is the perfect description of the United States in 1996. It is the best of times, but in many ways it is also the worst of times.

You don't have to be a wild-eyed optimist to concede that this has been an extraordinary century for the United States. In fact, some of the historians have called this the "American Century." I think in many ways it is a fair description. The United States has incredible achievements that we can rightfully be proud of.

First of all, we led the way in the defeat of the two great "isms" of this century: first, Nazism in World War II. I was born at the end of that conflict, and I did not experience it firsthand, but my mother and father told me many stories of what it was like to be in America during those years. They spoke of the anxiety and worry, of how it felt to get up on a Sunday morning and find out your country had been the victim of a surprise attack at a place

Christians in the Public Square

called Pearl Harbor, and what it actually felt like to be worried that your nation could lose that war, that we might actually be defeated and occupied by a foreign power. But I read in Winston Churchill's diary that he wrote that he had the soundest sleep of the war the night after Pearl Harbor because, as terrible as the event was, Churchill knew that once the United States was in the conflict, there was no doubt the western democracies would prevail—that with our economic might, our military might, and the bravery of our young men and women, the democracies would win that war. He knew "the American race," as he called us, better than we knew ourselves.

When that war was over and the American soldiers returned home, the whole country wanted to focus on domestic life, on getting our country moving again. Quite frankly, we were unable to do it because then we found ourselves in the great "stare-down" with the Soviet Union that came to be known as the Cold War. Again, answering the call, we drew a line in the sand in Europe and in Asia, and we said to the Russians and to the Chinese, "This far, and no further. We will protect freedom and liberty around the world."

During those years we spent hundreds of billions of dollars of our tax money to build the weapons systems, to do the foreign aid, and all the things we had to do to prevail in that conflict. If it was just the money we had spent, it wouldn't be all that big of a deal. This is a rich country; we could make the money up. But we also invested our sons in what sometimes appeared to be God-forsaken places such as Porkchop Hill and Da Nang and a hundred other places with names we have forgotten. Blood of our blood, flesh of our flesh, and they paid many, many times the ultimate price for liberty.

There were carpers and critics at the time who said it wasn't worth it, it was just a big misunderstanding between us and the Communists. I think history will judge that it was worth it, that it was a noble sacrifice, one of the most noble sacrifices of this century. Again, something we can be deeply proud of.

What about American values? American values are sweeping the globe. What happened in China a few years ago when the students revolted against their Communist masters? They didn't march through the streets carrying copies of the sayings of Mao or even the wisdom of Confucius. They marched through the streets with copies of our Declaration of Independence. They built papier mache models of our Statue of Liberty. It was American values they rallied to.

I read that when the Communists took power in Cambodia,

Being Salt and Light in America

one of the first things they did was to round up everybody who wore glasses and took them away and either killed them or imprisoned them. There was a logic behind what they were doing, because they felt that if you wore glasses it meant you read books, and if you read books, then maybe your mind was already infected with words such as "All men are created equal and endowed by their Creator with certain unalienable rights." There is not a tyrant in the world today whose head rests easy on his pillow for fear that his subjects have already been infected with those words.

What about the American economy in this century? From my Ross Perot charts we would see an economy that goes up and down; there are good times and bad, periods of recession and depression, periods of recovery, inflation, deflation, etc. But if we were to look at one long chart from 1900 until today, we would see a gently rising line of economic achievement. Our system of democratic capitalism has provided more jobs for more people than any system in the world. Socialism, by and large, is dying around the globe. It still prevails in a few congressional committees where they haven't fully discerned the meaning of the last election, or it has its adherents among the faculties of some universities, but by and large, people around the world are choosing free markets, free enterprise, the right to start a business, a job, and to achieve whatever you can for you and your family.

I could go on and on about America's achievements in this century. There are many, many more of them: the space program, our technological breakthroughs, the many things we have done in the medical area. Again, there is much to be proud of. But then, that is only half the story, because if it is the best of times, it is also the worst of times.

For about fifteen years now about two-thirds of the American people have been telling the pollsters that America is headed in the wrong direction. They said that when George Bush was in the White House and the Democrats controlled the Congress, and they're saying it today with Bill Clinton in the White House and the Republicans controlling the Congress. I believe that what those two-thirds of Americans are thinking about is not the economy or the military or our foreign policy. I think they are pondering on what is happening to the heart and soul of America. I believe they're thinking about the mother in South Carolina who strapped her two children in the backseat of a car and sent it to the bottom of a lake, or the six-year-old in Chicago who was thrown out of a window to his death by two ten-year-olds because he wouldn't shoplift for them, or the family in Los Angeles who took a wrong turn and before they could get off that street of

Christians in the Public Square

killers their three-year-old daughter was dead of sniper fire in their car. I think we all have a sense that America is one wrong turn away from a disaster.

You can measure a great nation in many different ways. You can measure it by the size of its GNP, the strength of its military, the gleam of its cities. By those measurements the United States is a great, great nation. But you can also measure a nation by how many of its children cry themselves to sleep. And the fact of the matter is that now in the United States too many of our children will cry themselves to sleep. Too many children are abandoned, too many children are without a father's arms to comfort them, too many children are exploited by drugs or pornography or sexual abuse. I think by that measurement America is in danger of becoming something quite less than a great nation.

What in the world has gone wrong, and what can we do as men and women of faith? The first thing that has gone wrong—and it certainly isn't very "in" to say it in today's America—is that we have forgotten God, and having forgotten God, we have unleashed the hounds of hell on our street and our neighborhoods and our communities. This is an incredibly ironic thing to happen in the United States, of all places. Lincoln called us the "almost chosen people." Every one of us has in our pockets or purses money that says "In God We Trust," and that phrase has become as valued as the money it is printed on. To listen to the cultural elites in Washington and around the country and in the media, you would think the greatest threat facing America is that Christian men and women may get into the public square and actually attempt to affect public policy. I believe the truth is the exact opposite—that unless men and women of faith get into the public square and stand for certain values, America will fall as surely as it would from economic collapse.

I believe you are the only ones who can explain to this nation why it is that only a virtuous people can remain free. I think you're the only ones who can explain to this nation that the family is God's chosen institution to raise children and to guarantee the most happiness to the most people. I believe you are the only ones who can explain to America the need for racial reconciliation based on the fact that we are all creatures of the same God. Without you in the public square to talk about those things, America is doomed.

I think the second thing that has happened is that we have separated the idea of virtue from liberty. There is a big argument going on about how Christian the Founding Fathers were. Some of them were Christians; some of them were deists; there were a few

Being Salt and Light in America

agnostics. There is a debate even in Christian circles about whether this was intended to be a Christian nation per se.

There should be no debate about this: Every one of our founders believed that only a virtuous people could remain free. The whole Constitution is written based on that idea. That is why we were given a limited government. The notion was that the virtue within us would restrain our passions, and we would not need an overweening, large government to prevent us from doing the things that we shouldn't do. Our consciences would do that; the virtue we embrace would do that. Yet today in 1996 the popular culture teaches our children that virtue is old-fashioned. Different strokes for different folks. If it feels good, do it. If that notion gains credence among the American people it will doom the democracy.

I was astonished a few months back to see the reaction to the death of Jerry Garcia, the leader of the band, The Grateful Dead. Some people liked their music; some did not. There is no accounting for taste. But what struck me was the reaction to Jerry Garcia's death, because he never escaped the sixties. He was a drug addict, an alcoholic, and he wrestled with those demons his entire life, and yet when he passed on to his reward, the culture in this country greeted his death as if a great American hero had left us. In fact, that night on the evening news it was among the first two or three stories. I saw senators walk out of committee hearings into the hallway to go to a bank of cameras to talk about how crushed they were that this great man had died. There is something wrong when Jerry Garcia is held up to great acclaim as somebody our children should look up to and should follow.

I suppose there is no better example of the virtue deficit this country increasingly wrestles with than the issue of abortion on demand. We have been subjected to a multimillion-dollar campaign to try to tell us that the highest American value is choice. That's ludicrous. That has never been the highest American value. It has always been what we choose, not the act of choosing that matters. We don't say to the child pornographer, "Well, that's your choice if you want to use child pornography." We don't say to the wife-abuser, "That's up to you what you and your wife do in the privacy of your own home. That's your decision. We're not going to say anything about it." No, we have made a decision as a civilized nation that we won't tolerate those things. It would be my hope that sometime soon we would make a decision as a civilized nation that we won't tolerate 1.5 million abortions a year.

Christians in the Public Square

We have had this debate before. We had it more than one hundred years ago. I reread many, many times the Lincoln-Douglas debates, and I have concluded after reading them that Senator Douglas was the original pro-choice advocate. Senator Douglas went all over the state of Illinois, and his arguments really boiled down to this, as horrendous as it sounds today: "I can't prove that black men and women are people under the Constitution, and not knowing whether they're people, I have no right to force my view on anyone else. If Alabama wants to be a slave state," Douglas said, "that's up to them. Illinois can be a free state. If my neighbor wants to own a slave, that's his decision. No one is forcing me to own one." Lincoln listened to those arguments, and he said, "Senator Douglas, you would give choice to everyone except the person it matters the most to, the slave." Today's pro-choice advocates would give choice to everyone except those it matters the most to, our unborn children.

I know the abortion culture seems insurmountable. It has the high ground in American society. It controls the media. It controls the universities. It controls the courts. I really believe in my heart that, as strong as it seems, that fortress of abortion on demand will fall a lot sooner than any of us think.

I want to encourage you and to tell you not to run from this battle. Recently I was going through some old quotes that I keep around to remind me of some truths I think we all should remember. One was written by John Quincy Adams twenty years before the Civil War:

> The world, the flesh, and all the devils in hell are arrayed against any man who now in this North American union shall dare to join the standard of Almighty God to put down the African slave trade. What can I upon the verge of my seventy-fourth birthday, with a shaking hand, a darkening eye, a drowsy brain, and with all my faculties dropping from me one by one as the teeth are dropping from my head, what can I do for the cause of God and man? Yet my conscience presses me on. Let me but die upon the breach.

Adams did die a few hours after a heated debate on the floor of the Congress. Henry Clay held his hand. Congressman Lincoln made the final funeral arrangements. Daniel Webster wrote the inscription on the casket. These were giants among us, and every one of them served their country because they were first and foremost God-fearing men who felt an obligation to do so. We are their children. We are called to follow the standard they have left for us.

Being Salt and Light in America

When I was in the Reagan White House I got to do some incredible things for a Southern Baptist boy from Northern Kentucky. Nobody in my family had ever finished high school, let alone gone on to college and then law school. There I found myself sitting at the Cabinet table of the United States. I had lunch every Monday with the President and flew on Air Force One. It was great stuff to do. I had a ball. I'd be lying to you if I told you those things didn't matter to me. But when I'm on the road traveling around the country, and I'm in some hotel after talking to a group, and the lights go off at night and my head hits the pillow, I'm not thinking about Ronald Reagan or Air Force One. I'm thinking about what happened at Calvary, about the incredible love of a God who would save even a sinner like me. I'm thinking about the love of my wife, Carol, of what it sounds like when I get home and the first words that I hear when I come in the door are my son Zachary saying, "Dad, let's wrestle." Or what my daughter looked like when she went out on her first date, or for that matter, what I looked like when she went out on her first date. I'm not unique in that regard. Those are the things you care about, too. Those are the things that millions of Americans still believe in.

Fight for those things. Stand for those things. Teach your children about those things. Only support candidates who are willing, without shame or embarrassment, to defend those things. If you will do that, then I am absolutely convinced that some day soon every one of us again without hesitation will be able to say that America is a shining city upon a hill.

*Challenges
We Face*

WHEN CHRISTIANS DON'T MAKE A DIFFERENCE

By David P. Gushee

I have the unpleasant assignment of delivering bad news—the bad news of what happens "When Christians Don't Make a Difference" in the political life of the nations in which God has placed us. Surely it would be a happier experience to relate the good news of what happens when Christians *do* make a difference in politics. But then I feel certain that the unpleasant story I must tell is a story that very much needs to be told—and heard—today. It is a story so tragic, with Christian failure so glaring, and with consequences so horrendous, that it needs to be burned into the consciousness of every Christian person who walks this earth in the years that still remain before Christ returns.

The story I tell is of Christian political failure in relation to Adolf Hitler and Nazism.

In telling you this story, I could address three related but quite distinct periods. I could focus on the period running from 1939 to 1945—the World War II years. During these years the Nazi regime initiated an international conflagration which ultimately left fifty-five million people dead, including six million Jews, victims of what has come to be called the Holocaust. In my book, *The Righteous Gentiles of the Holocaust,* I have told the story of how Christians in Europe responded to the Nazi effort to capture and kill their Jewish neighbors. Their mixed response—from rescuing Jews to doing nothing to participating in their

Christians in the Public Square

murder—is of extreme moral importance.[1] But this is not the story I tell today.

Alternatively, I could focus on the period from 1933 to 1939 in Germany itself. On January 30, 1933, Adolf Hitler was named Chancellor of Germany. Though personally he had nothing but contempt for democracy as a political system, he had ascended through the democratic process. He and his party had won sufficient popular support to gain him this critical post in the German government. Within six months he had destroyed German democracy and established himself as *der Fuhrer,* dictator of what would soon become a totalitarian state. The account of how Christians responded to the consolidation of Hitler's dictatorship, to his policies, and especially to his efforts to control and nazify the churches of Germany (the so-called German Church Struggle)—is also a compelling and important one. But it too has been told many times before.[2]

Instead, I want to reflect primarily on Christian *political* failure during the Nazi years. By the time of World War II, most Christians were not faced with issues of politics. By then very few Europeans had any opportunity whatsoever to affect the nature of the Nazi regime or the shape of its policies. The only choice available to the Christians of Europe under Nazi occupation was whether or not to risk their lives opposing this murderous and evil regime. Here we are beyond politics. Here we have a test of personal and community character.

To a lesser extent the same was true during the German Church Struggle in the 1930s, after Hitler consolidated his power. By the middle of 1933 democratic politics was dead in Germany, though not everyone recognized it at the time. The issue for Christians in Germany who recognized the true nature of the Nazi regime became simply whether or not they had the courage, at the risk of their freedom and possibly of their lives, to resist. Again, for the most part we are beyond politics, for politics had already failed.

Politics failed in the period between the birth of the Nazi party in 1919 and the ascension of Adolf Hitler to the chancellorship of Germany in 1933. It was in these fateful fourteen years that the Nazis moved from a rightist fringe group of fifty-five people to a mass national party able to garner 33 percent of the popular vote in November 1932, the last free and fair parliamentary elections in Germany until after the war. This 33 percent was enough to win Adolf Hitler the chancellor's office, from which he proceeded to dismantle German democracy and ultimately to destroy millions of human beings. So let us

When Christians Don't Make a Difference

concentrate our attention on what happened when Germany's Christians did not make a difference in politics—and thus allowed, and even helped, Adolf Hitler become the leader of a great European nation, a leader who would plunge that nation into utter darkness and take the world with him.

The Postwar German Crisis and the Nazi Response

A profound and politically very dangerous crisis wracked Germany after World War I. It was a time that called for farsighted, discerning, authentically Christian involvement in politics. Tragically, this kind of involvement was lacking. On the whole, there was nothing distinctively Christian about the response of Germany's Christian churches, leaders, politicians, and rank-and-file members to the crisis that faced their nation. This failure to offer a distinct witness, to rise above sinful, yet predictable, human responses to national crises—such as fear, pride, selfishness, and hate—was the fundamental Christian political failure of this period in German history.

It is indeed impossible to understand the rise of Nazism without a grasp of the extraordinary crisis that afflicted Germany after the loss of World War I. In autumn 1918 Germany's military collapsed after four years of war. The surrender came as a shock to the people of this proud nation. They had trusted the assurances of their leaders that, despite reversals along the way, the war ultimately would be won. Now nearly two million of Germany's young men had died in vain. For comparison, consider our own profound and ongoing national trauma concerning the loss of the Vietnam war and of a "mere" 57,000 soldiers.

On November 9, 1918, a revolution forced the abdication of Kaiser Wilhelm II. The only political system that most Germans had ever known was swept away. The successor to the second Reich was a fledgling parliamentary democracy that came to be called the Weimar Republic. Weimar was structured along lines similar to that of the victorious western democracies, but it was never to have anything resembling their stability. One reason for its chronic weakness was that its very legitimacy was bitterly disputed. While politically progressive forces such as the Social Democrats and Liberals created and supported Weimar, a large bloc of socially and culturally conservative Germans, including most Christians, yearned for the restoration of the Kaiser and for a past that was never to return.[3]

Contempt for the Weimar regime was intensified profoundly during 1919 when the government was forced to accept the terms of the Versailles Treaty. This peace settlement (popularly known

Christians in the Public Square

in Germany as the *Schanvertrag*—the treaty of dishonor) saddled Germany with total blame for the war, imposed severe reparations, restricted the size of the German military, and deprived the nation of significant territories. The young democracy was irreparably damaged by its association with this hated treaty, which deepened the cultural despair and political polarization of Germany.

Revolutionary activity on both the left and the right grew more intense. Many feared a Communist revolution, as had occurred just the year before in Russia and which the Communists were indeed hoping to extend to Germany. This fear was fed by particularly convulsive political instability and the constant turnover of governments at the state level. In Bavaria, for example, left- and right-wing coups occurred so frequently during the immediate postwar years as to have been almost routine. Yet political instability of this magnitude is serious business. It is no coincidence that Bavaria is where Adolf Hitler got his start.

The Nazi party, which Hitler did not actually found but came to lead in the early 1920s, was but one of several small but vocal extreme right-wing parties active in Germany at this time. It is a truism of politics that extreme conditions produce extreme reactions. National trauma produces politicians who reflect that trauma. Witness a Vladimir Zhirinovsky in Russia. During such periods people look for strong leaders who can identify with their suffering, articulate their frustrations, offer a cogent explanation of why things are so bad, and promise to make things better.

The rightist parties in Germany at this time essentially shared a common script. Hitler's demonic genius lay in his unique skill in articulating it. This ability was what primarily propelled him to the leadership of the Nazi party, of the rightist camp, and finally of the nation. But the script itself was not unique to Hitler.

Essentially it went like this: We Germans are a humiliated people. Our young men have died by the millions, and in vain. We are the victims of incomprehensible international injustice. We have had our sovereignty violated and have been emasculated as a nation. Our territory has been stripped from us. Our military has been decimated. We suffer severe economic deprivation. We are being ruled by a weak and illegitimate government. Our culture is being perverted by avant-garde foreign influences. Our nation is no longer our own but is overrun by strangers who seek our harm.

Why has all this happened? According to Hitler and most of the right-wing parties, the answer was very simple. It was the Jews. Imagining a vast international Jewish conspiracy, Hitler

When Christians Don't Make a Difference

argued that everything could be explained by this conspiracy. The war was lost because of the Jews. Germany's Jews had been disloyal during the war and had stabbed the nation in the back. Jewish war profiteers had made big money off the war at the expense of the war effort and the average German. The Versailles Treaty was imposed by the western nations, all of which were under the control of a Jewish cabal. The Weimar government was essentially a Jewish creation and also was under Jewish control. Communism, the most severe political threat, was for Hitler also a Jewish invention. Germany's postwar economic problems were also to be traced to Jewish business and finance, both at home and abroad. Jews, finally, controlled the media, Hitler argued, and were responsible for the cultural "perversions" that one could witness in such places as Berlin.

This absolutely absurd diagnosis was accompanied by similarly radical solutions. Here I draw primarily from the first Nazi party platform, which appeared in 1920.[4] The platform essentially argues that Germany must refuse to cooperate with the international community in the enforcement of provisions of Versailles. It should renounce the war-guilt clause, rebuild its military, and reclaim its territories. It should restore national racial purity and well-being by preventing any non-German immigration and by expelling any immigrants who arrived after the start of World War I. It must establish citizenship on a racial basis, thus disenfranchising the Jews and stripping them of any public role or presence; additionally, Jewish economic power and resources must be reduced or eliminated (this point is implicit rather than explicit in the platform itself).

Hitler's goal at this time was (at the very least) the removal of the Jews from Germany altogether.[5] Germany's government should assume central control over institutions of culture, such as the media, to cleanse them of their corruption and of foreign influences. As for German religious life, "positive Christianity" must be promoted, but only insofar as it is consistent with "the moral feelings of the German race" and is stripped of any trace of the "Jewish-materialist spirit." A strong central government was required to accomplish all of these goals.

The Christian Response to Nazism and its Program

There it is, the heart of the published Nazi party platform of 1920. How did Germany's Christians respond to this agenda and the party that articulated it?

Here is the bad news: Many of them liked what they heard. What could they possibly have liked, we might ask?

• They liked the nationalism, the emphasis on the military, the

Christians in the Public Square

promise to reclaim German territories, and the entire tone of defiant German pride;
• They liked the concern for their economic well-being and the promise to suppress those forces which were supposedly costing Germans their livelihood in disastrous economic times;
• They liked the tone of strength and will and the promise to use centralized political power to restore order and suppress both political and social chaos in Germany;
• They liked the strong anti-communism, for they feared communism profoundly;
• They liked the anti-immigrant emphasis, for they too did not gladly welcome non-Germans, especially non-Christian Germans, into their nation;
• They liked the cultural conservatism, and the promise to suppress avant-garde, corrupt, and alien cultural expression;
• They liked the idea of "positive Christianity" and the promise of a protection of Christian cultural and political privileges;
• All too many liked the Jewish conspiracy theory and at least some of the promises of how to deal with Jews in Germany.

It is critical at this point to remember that the Nazis never won an electoral majority in a fair national election in Germany. At their peak, in July 1932, they won 37.2 percent of the vote. It never can be accurately said that most German Christians voted for Hitler and his party during their rise to power. But enough did—just enough. A majority is not always required to win political power, even in our system. Witness the presidential election of 1992. In what was an overwhelmingly Christian nation, at least by baptism and self-identification, just over one-third of the people volunteered their support for Adolf Hitler. They looked at the same published agenda we have been looking at here, and they liked it better than any of the alternatives. And so Hitler came to power.

Sources of Christian Political Failure—and Lessons for Us

This analysis forces us to ask a prior question: Why were Germany's Christians so unprepared to respond in a biblical manner, a distinctively Christian manner, to the political crisis that swept Germany? How could so many of them have been so open to supporting Adolf Hitler and his party? The reasons extend deep into the history of German Christianity, and are relevant to us as well. I will name five reasons for their susceptibility to this tragic political failure, and consider implications for our own political involvement and political vision today.

They were susceptible because of their longstanding

When Christians Don't Make a Difference

identification of traditional German cultural values with Christianity.

The established German churches (I focus primarily here on the Protestant side) had enjoyed a privileged cultural position for centuries. The German Evangelical Church dominated the religious landscape—forty million of the nation's sixty-five million people in 1910 were members of one of the twenty-eight regional Evangelical Church bodies.[6] On the whole, the German Evangelical Church and its leaders were middle class and profoundly culturally conservative. They were nationalistic and had supported the monarchy with unquestioning loyalty. When Kaiser Wilhelm fell, they were horrified. The political chaos of the Weimar years offended their sense of order. The cultural freedom and experimentation of that period offended their sense of decency. They wanted a return to the *ancien regime,* the old order, which they looked upon with wistful remembrance. Their values were patriotism, hard work, thriftiness, loyalty, obedience, moral decency, and honor. These were "family values" Christians of the first order. They feared that such values were rapidly draining out of German life.

Many of these traditional values were, and are, commendable. The mistake these Christians made was in collapsing their understanding of Christian faith and morality into total identification with these values and a social order that they believed embodied them. In doing so they failed to embrace other important biblical moral norms such as the requirement to be concerned for the well-being of the stranger and the alien (Ex. 22:21; Luke 10:25-37), the call to peacemaking and to a faith that transcends national loyalties (Matt. 5:9, 21-26; Rom. 12:9-21), and the demand for social justice (Isa. 1:17; Amos 5:21-24; Mic. 6:8). This identification of their own conservative cultural traditions with Christianity left them readily susceptible to manipulation by Hitler, who was no Christian by any stretch of the imagination. Indeed, Hitler actually hated Christianity and made plans during his regime for its destruction. But during the critical years in which he rose to power he skillfully articulated the churches' cultural conservatism, claimed it as his own, and thus won many Christians to his side.

Far too frequently we Christians do the same thing today. We pick a cluster of cultural values—radical, liberal, moderate, or conservative—and baptize these as Christian. We vote for politicians who articulate those cultural values and are especially enthusiastic about those who skillfully baptize these values in a

Christians in the Public Square

Christian vocabulary. Then we offer these politicians our uncritical and unquestioning support. When we do this we fall prey to a cultural captivity that robs the church of any ability to separate the wheat from the chaff, the biblical values from the unbiblical values. We lose our political independence. We become mere outposts of whatever branch of the culture we happen to occupy. Frequently this is so transparent that it weakens, if not destroys, any distinctive public Christian witness we might have. It is the Bible that is to set our political, cultural, and moral agenda, not the culture. The point is obvious, but it is far easier said than done.

They were susceptible because of their political and legal status as established churches and their self-interested desire to retain this status.

The German Evangelical Church was politically established, not just culturally established. Ever since the Reformation, which was protected by the German princes region by region, there had been a formal alliance—one might say a marriage—between German Protestantism and the state. The state collected taxes to support the church and provided subsidies for churches and parochial schools. Christianity was taught in the public schools as a matter of course. While church and state were seen as occupying separate realms or spheres of influence, they were viewed both by church and state as inseparable allies, as partners who together led German society.

The fall of the Kaiser appeared to threaten this cozy arrangement. The established churches were especially concerned about the hostility directed their way by some of the Social Democrats, Liberals, and Communists and by those they represented. The church had for some time been having trouble reaching urban workers and was increasingly identified by such folks as a middle-class, conservative institution unworthy of mandated tax support from the entire populace. Published attacks by political liberals on the church and its privileges terrified and enraged church leaders and many laypeople.[7] Christians feared that Germany would become a liberal, atheistic, godless, socialist or even Communist state that would seek to destroy the church, as was happening in Russia.

The main political goal of the established churches became the maintenance of their privileged position. Hitler helped himself enormously with the churches by promising to support that goal. As noted, the Nazi party platform articulated its support for "positive Christianity" and "freedom for all religious

When Christians Don't Make a Difference

denominations in the State." When Hitler came to power he assured the churches that they were "the most important factor safeguarding our national heritage," and their teachings "the basis of our whole morality." He promised that he would "assure [the churches] the influence" due them as the institutions providing "the unshakable foundations of our people's ethical and moral life."[8]

These were just the promises church leaders had been seeking. Success was at hand! All but a few failed to notice that the Nazis explicitly declared religious liberty subordinate to the "moral feelings of the German race" as interpreted by the Nazi party. In other words, there would be religious liberty for any religion the Nazis believed acceptable. They failed to see that for Hitler an acceptable German Christianity would need to be stripped of its Jewish heritage and any Jewish converts in leadership positions. They failed to anticipate that the promised privileging of the church would be accompanied by an assault on the human rights and religious liberty of their Jewish neighbors. The church was, on the whole, all too willing to trade its allegiance to Hitler, or at least its neutrality, for this mess of pottage.

The desire to receive political privileges at the hands of the state also is a temptation that Christians in this country face today. While it is ruled out under our system for any church to be formally established, for decades the informal establishment of Protestant Christianity was the reality throughout most of the nation, and remains so in some regions of our land. However, since the 1960s this informal establishment has in many ways been destroyed both by the culture and the law.

As a Baptist, I believe in the disestablishment of religion as articulated in the "establishment clause" of the First Amendment. Disestablishment is good for the church and for the state. But today we see a fierce counterreaction among many evangelical Christians to what has occurred over these recent decades. I am among those who believe that a portion of this counterreaction is justifiable, for it is at least arguable that both culturally and legally we have witnessed not mere disestablishment but the de facto establishment of the quasireligion known as secularism, accompanied by a hostility to Christianity.

We can leave this particular argument to another day. The lesson to be drawn from the period we are considering is the following: Christians absolutely must avoid the temptation to see politics merely as the arena in which the self-interest of the church (or our particular branch or version of the church) is promoted and

Christians in the Public Square

protected. We absolutely must avoid the seductive politician who would promise to provide privileges for us that are inconsistent with our nation's constitutional principles.

This is just what the German churches did. They sought primarily to promote and protect their institutional self-interest and then accepted the false promises of a politician who said he would protect and advance those interests for them. As the German pastor/theologian/martyr Dietrich Bonhoeffer so clearly articulated, self-interest is not an adequate Christian political ethic. Bonhoeffer argued that the church, like its Lord Jesus, must be for others, not for itself. A church that is consumed by self-interest is no different from any other player in the political arena. A church that is consumed by self-interest will have neither time nor attention to spare for what is being done to "the least of these" (Matt. 25:31f). A political agenda or policy does not have to negatively affect our institutional self-interest to be of concern to us. Hitler's proposed disenfranchisement of the Jews was one such policy. Self-interest said "leave that one alone." Christian principles said to reject, denounce, and resist any such policy. This the church did not do, even during the German Church Struggle of the 1930s.

They were susceptible because a long history of Christian anti-Semitism left the church open to Nazi racial and political anti-Semitism.

Looking back, most of us find anti-Semitism and its ultimate fruit, the Holocaust, to be the most obviously evil dimension of Hitler's ideology and policies. A virulent and vicious anti-Semitism is clearly visible throughout the published documents and speeches of Nazi leaders from the party's very beginning. Our earlier review of the Nazi party platform illustrated this. Explicit and total contempt for the Jewish people courses through the documents Nazism has left to us throughout its entire wretched existence.

Because all human beings are made in the image of God (Gen. 1:26-27), and are equally and immeasurably valuable in His sight, anti-Semitism or any other form of racial hatred is sufficient to disqualify a political party or political leader from Christian consideration. Whatever other elements or stances might characterize such a leader or party, racism in and of itself nullifies their legitimacy. No supposedly Christian candidate can emit even the whiff of racism.

Do Christians know this today? Certainly such a belief was not widely shared among Christians in 1920s Germany—quite the contrary. Helmut Gollwitzer, who became an opponent of Nazism,

When Christians Don't Make a Difference

has pointed out that anti-Semitism was part and parcel of "average Protestant" life in Germany in the period we are discussing. It was routine to believe that Jews were an economic, political, and religious menace to Germany, and that their influence must, at the very least, be restrained. The party's promise to disenfranchise Jews was seen as "a matter worth consideration" by decent and respectable Christian folks.[9]

The long history of Christian anti-Semitism, which took deep root in Germany but not only there, prepared the way. This anti-Semitism resurged during the 1920s. It was not only Hitler and his party who promoted it. When this occurred, an authentic Christianity had the responsibility to stop it cold. Christians should have known without a doubt that his vicious anti-Semitism disqualified Hitler from serious political consideration. But many did not. Instead, his anti-Semitism either did not harm him or actually helped him with most Christian voters. This is abhorrent. Yet I am sad to say that such failure continues to be repeated in our own great nation, even on this side of the Holocaust.

They were susceptible because the erosion of thoughtful theological orthodoxy left the churches open to theological and moral confusion concerning the true nature of Hitler and his party.

I cannot fail to mention that Germany was the headquarters of classical theological liberalism, and that this movement was in the last stages of its ascendancy in Germany during the period we are considering. I am not the first to suggest that this theological liberalism—with its loss of confidence in biblical authority, its loss of commitment to biblical fidelity, its faltering belief in the transcendent, holy God who took flesh in Jesus Christ the Jew, its weakened sense of the distinct identity and mission of the church, its openness to all manner of theological experimentation, and its lack of spiritual vitality—weakened the resistance of the German churches to Nazism. Such an accusation is not original to me but emerged from within Germany itself, from such theological giants as Karl Barth and others who became involved in the Confessing Church movement during the years of the Nazi regime.

In hindsight, it seems so clear. All anyone really needs to do is one careful reading of the Nazi platform or of Hitler's 1925 autobiography *Mein Kampf*. Within these pages alone there is more than enough evidence to establish—by 1925!—the utter irreconcilability of Nazism and any authentic Christianity. But for the reasons we are discussing the churches failed to understand what they were dealing with in a man such as Adolf Hitler. They were unable to discern that they were not looking at a Christ but an antichrist. They were bamboozled, fooled, seduced.

Christians in the Public Square

They were theologically undiscerning and politically naive.
Many contemporary evangelical writers, such as David Wells and Mark Noll, warn us of similar dangers in Christian life today. So often we treat intellectual effort generally, and theological reflection in particular, as optional luxuries rather than fundamentals of Christian discipleship. The result is intellectually and theologically flabby churches that lack the ability to tell truth from falsehood, orthodoxy from heresy, authentic from counterfeit Christianity. In "normal times" such a problem is bad enough. In times of social stress and political crisis it can be devastating. Behold Adolf Hitler—family-values candidate, defender of the church, upholder of morality, savior of the nation. Behold the consequences of Christian theological negligence and intellectual decay.

In summary: German Christians failed because they carried into the crisis years a badly truncated political vision. This distorted vision left them susceptible to the devilish charms of Adolf Hitler.

Germany's Christians failed to prevent the rise of Adolf Hitler. Surely this was the worst Christian political failure of the twentieth century. I have argued that while massive national trauma was the context of this failure, its roots run deeper, to an uncritical cultural Christianity, to institutional self-interestedness, inherited anti-Semitism, and theological confusion. Surely other tributaries could be identified. The net result was the development of a deeply distorted and misshapen political vision. This truncated vision led some in the church to believe that they could, without contradiction, be committed Christians and committed supporters of a man and a party characterized by racism, anti-Semitism, nationalism, militarism, xenophobia, and a hatred for democracy.

How frightening this is! How frightening that Christians can so easily be fooled. How frightening that, if a politician pushes certain buttons to which many of us instinctively respond, we immediately lose full use of the Scriptures and of our critical faculties. Christians must watch out for those who claim the mantle of the church and of Christianity on the basis of a wildly distorted "Christian scorecard" of positions, a scorecard that fails to reflect a holistic biblical vision for political life.

All of this leads to the most disturbing observation of all. The question I have been addressing—"What happens when Christians don't make a difference" in politics—may be miscast. Let me say it plainly. The rise of Hitler is inconceivable apart from the "difference" that "Christians" at their worst did, in fact, make

When Christians Don't Make a Difference

through the centuries prior to the rise of Nazism and during that rise itself. It was Christians who developed the acculturated Germanic Christianity, the churchly self-interestedness, the religious anti-Semitism, and the theological liberalism we have been discussing. And let us not forget that Hitler himself was a baptized Christian, a lapsed Catholic, and one who during his rise and his reign manipulated Christian concepts and vocabulary for his own evil purposes. Hitler hated the church, but he hated it as an estranged son, not as a foreigner. His name could be found on the church roll.

So we must not understand the political life of our own or any nation merely as the struggle between a purer-than-the-driven-snow Christianity on the one hand and evil non-Christian movements and ideologies on the other. In predominantly Christian nations, such as our own, the struggle is quite frequently between competing versions of Christianity, not always between Christianity and some alternative faith or ideology. Sometimes it is perversions of Christian faith that pose the greatest danger. We Christians have plenty of reason for humility, and are called by our Lord to a constant spirit of self-examination and repentance as we engage in politics or any other dimension of life (Matt. 7:1-5). We must recognize that sometimes the finger of blame needs to be pointed directly at ourselves rather than at some perceived enemy of the faith who resides beyond our gate.

We learn from the tragic story of Germany and Hitler that politics matters. We learn that there is no substitute for Christian involvement in politics. But we also learn that Christians must be discerning about what *kind* of political involvement truly accords with the will of God. Our citizenship responsibilities are immense. In an election year, of all years, we should be on our knees, praying for God's aid in fulfilling those responsibilities.

Endnotes

[1] David P. Gushee, *The Righteous Gentiles of the Holocaust: A Christian Interpretation* (Minneapolis: Augsburg Fortress, 1994).

[2] See John S. Conway, *The Nazi Persecution of the Churches. 1933-45* (New York: Basic Books, 1968); Franklin H. Littell and Hubert G. Locke, eds., *The German Church Struggle and the Holocaust* (San Francisco: Mellen Research Univ. Press, 1990).

[3] Victoria Barnett, *For the Soul of the People* (New York: Oxford University Press, 1992), 9.

[4] For the text of the 1920 Nazi platform, see J. Noakes and G. Pridham, eds., *Nazism* (New York: Schocken Books, 1983), 14-16.

Christians in the Public Square

[5]Hitler articulated this goal in his first extant political writing, dated 1919. For that text, see Noakes and Pridham, *Nazism,* 13. Some have argued that this statement should be interpreted as the intention to murder the Jews, not just deport them.

[6]Barnett, *For the Soul of the People,* 12.

[7]Ibid., 14.

[8]Quoted in Eberhard Bethge, *Dietrich Bonhoeffer* (New York: Harper & Row, 1977), 202.

[9]Quoted in Barnett, *For the Soul of the People,* 15.

THE FIGHT FOR RELIGIOUS LIBERTY

By Jay Sekulow

PART I. *An Overview: From Toleration to Respect*

The efforts to privatize, marginalize, and trivialize the impact that people of faith (particularly Christians) have on our culture has received a stinging rebuke. Perhaps the dominant cultural elitists who most often engage in this privatization process could handle the rebuke more easily if it came from one associated with the Religious Right. Interestingly, however, the rebuke comes from one who most often sides with these cultural elitists on the substantive moral issues. Like a voice crying in the wilderness, Stephen L. Carter's *The Culture of Disbelief*[1] is a refreshing examination of the role of people of faith in society today. Recognizing at the outset that many in contemporary America treat those with religious convictions as irrelevant in the marketplace of ideas, Carter asks his readers to reexamine their own perceptions and misconceptions of the role of religious people in American public life. Richard John Neuhaus, in his review of *The Culture of Disbelief,* applauds Carter's efforts, calling him "a voice for sanity and justice in a political culture that is at a deadly war with itself."[2]

The central thesis running throughout Carter's book is that liberals, whether in the media, the legal establishment, or the political arena, have overtly trivialized religious belief and devotion so significantly that popular culture considers neither to

Christians in the Public Square

be worthy of respect or serious attention. Carter writes,
> One sees a trend in our political and legal culture toward treating religious belief as arbitrary and unimportant, a trend supported by a rhetoric that implies that there is something wrong with religious devotion. More and more, our culture seems to take the position that believing deeply in the tenets of one's faith represents a kind of mystical irrationality, something they feel public-spirited American citizens would do better to avoid."[3]

Carter pointedly establishes that the trivializing factor aimed at religious people is wrong.

"We err," Carter writes,
> when we presume that religious motives are likely to be illiberal, and we compound our error when we insist that the devout should keep their religious ideas—whether good or bad—to themselves. We do no credit to the ideal of religious freedom when we talk as though religious belief is something of which public-spirited adults should be ashamed.[4]

In the forward to the paperback edition of *The Culture of Disbelief* (1994), Carter notes what he calls the "good news" that has taken place since the publication of the hardcover edition. "There has been remarkable evidence of a change in some of the conditions" described in the earlier edition of the book.[5]

Carter then briefly discusses the United States Supreme Court case *Lamb's Chapel v. Center Moriches Union Free School District*.[6] *Lamb's Chapel* involved a church that desired to rent out a school auditorium for six consecutive Wednesday evenings to show a film series produced by Focus on the Family called *Turn Your Heart Towards Home*. The meetings were to be free of charge and open to the community. The school district refused to grant permission to show the film because it approached contemporary family issues from an admittedly "religious perspective." The Supreme Court held that the school district engaged in unconstitutional viewpoint discrimination. Carter appropriately applauds the Court's decision.

No doubt Carter is correct in referring to the decision as "good news." Further, the underlying reasons put forth by the New York Attorney General for censoring the film strongly support Carter's thesis. In their brief, the Attorney General argued fervently that the suppression of private religious speakers actually advances the

The Fight for Religious Liberty

public good, stating, "Religious advocacy serves the community only in the eyes of its adherents and yields a benefit only to those who already believe."[7]

The Attorney General's trivializing of religious values met with sharp questioning from the Supreme Court's Justice Scalia. This portion of the underlying argument is worth reviewing.

Justice Scalia: "You are here representing both respondents [the school board and the state of New York] .... In this argument, and the Attorney General of New York, in his brief defending...the New York rule says that 'religious advocacy serves the community only in the eyes of its adherents and yields a benefit only to those who already believe.' Does New York State—I grew up in New York, and in those days they used to have a tax exemption for religious property. Is that still there?"

Counsel: "Yes, your Honor, it still is."

Justice Scalia: "But they changed their view apparently, that—"

Counsel: "Well, your Honor—"

Justice Scalia: "You see—it used to be thought that—that religion—it didn't matter what religion, but it—some code of morality always went with it and was thought, you know, what was called a God-fearing person might be less likely to mug me and rape my sister. That apparently is not the view of New York anymore."

Counsel: "Well, I'm not sure that that's—"

Justice Scalia: "Has this new regime worked very well?"[8]

The answer to Justice Scalia's question, as Stephen Carter has attested to, is that the new regime has not worked very well at all, and it never will. The effort of the Attorney General of the state of New York to privatize and censor from the marketplace of ideas religious faith and moral values will lead to serious negative consequences. The call for a renewal of faith-based values being used to address contemporary culture issues is gaining a wide hearing across confessional and political lines.

While individuals such as John Neuhaus have been pointing to the debris left in our society when religious values are stripped from the public square, it is refreshing to see similar words penned by Stephen Carter. Even a cursory review of *The Culture of Disbelief* will establish that its words are penned by an author who cannot be labeled a "conservative" or as one who is affiliated with the Christian Right. Stephen Carter is the William Nelson

Christians in the Public Square

Cromwell Professor of Law at Yale University and is among the nation's leading experts on constitutional law. Carter is also a Christian who is liberal in his social views on abortion and homosexual rights. Carter has done us a great service, and we should welcome with anticipation his views in the marketplace of ideas. As conservative evangelical Christians, our views will differ with some of those raised in the book, but we should appreciate the honesty Carter has brought to the debate.

Carter's assertion that the role of religious people can be vital in the debate over social issues is now trumpeted by leading liberal politicians. It was, after all, President Clinton who brought national attention to the book after he read an advance copy while vacationing at Martha's Vineyard. As George Wiegel, president of the Ethics and Public Policy Center, has so aptly stated, "For we may see, in certain signs of these times, a new public recognition of the realities of religious conviction in America and a new willingness to concede a place for religiously based moral argument in the American Public Square."[9]

Undoubtedly, Carter has brought the debate involving the role of people of faith in our body politic to new life. Fred Barnes, the former senior editor of *The New Republic,* noted that when David Wilhelm, former chairman of the Democratic National Committee, spoke at the national convention of the Christian Coalition, "he made a significant concession. He stressed that religious values are fine and legitimate as roots of political views."[10] Yet, perhaps the greatest concession of David Wilhelm was not so much what he said, but rather the fact that he chose to attend and address a significant meeting of the Religious Right. This shows, I believe, that as a movement, our views are being more than simply tolerated in the public square. Carter himself seeks more than toleration of religious perspectives. The dedication page of *The Culture of Disbelief* speaks volumes as to what Carter is seeking. "For Leah Cristina and Andrew David, who should be able to live in a world that *respects* your choices instead of tolerating them. God Bless."[11] (emphasis mine).

In seeking to gain respect for religious viewpoints, Carter has contributed much. Michael Horowitz, senior fellow at The Manhattan Institute, properly acknowledges the contribution Carter has made in "seeking to legitimate the political activism of a community with whose general views he broadly disagrees."[12] This does not mean, of course, that *The Culture of Disbelief* is not without legitimate criticism. As will be discussed later, Richard Land, president of the Christian Life Commission of the Southern Baptist Convention, and Professor Phillip E. Johnson of the

The Fight for Religious Liberty

University of California Berkeley point to inconsistencies in some of the ways in which Carter addressed key issues of the day.

Nonetheless, Carter, with significant intellectual integrity, has reasserted the need for at least acceptance of religiously motivated viewpoints being heard. Significantly, Carter advocates this position even on those moral issues on which he has strong disagreement with the Religious Right. For instance, although Carter clearly favors abortion rights, he points out that

> when Martin Luther King, Jr. declared in his 'Letter From Birmingham City Jail' that a 'just law is a man-made code that squares with the moral law or the law of God,' he was not bandying words; he was stating a bedrock commitment to the authority of God as *superior* to the authority of the state, a commitment on which much of the civil rights movement explicitly and enthusiastically rested. Nowadays, such commitments are evidently suspect, the mark of a fanatic, especially when urged in service of positions often described as right wing; consider the popular image of the pro-life movement. But our culture cannot be so hypocritical in its protestations of religious freedom as to endorse the intervention of the church against the state only in pursuit of expressly liberal ends.[13]

The role of religious-based institutions in historic and contemporary politics has been well documented.[14] From the abolitionists to the civil rights movement, religious values have shaped many of the significant cultural and moral issues of our history. As James W. Skillen, director of the Association for Public Justice, has observed,

> Few movements have shaped contemporary American politics as powerfully as has the Civil Rights movement that reached its height in the 1960s. Much of the vision, motivation, endurance and strategy of that movement is rooted in churches—especially African-American churches. The National Association for the Advancement of Colored People, the Southern Christian Leadership Conference, and many other organizations dedicated to overcoming racial discrimination were built on the only independent stronghold that many blacks knew—the church.[15]

Political correctness should not be a basis upon which to exclude the religious dissenter from the marketplace. Both sides of the political spectrum would do well to heed Carter's advice which

Christians in the Public Square

echoes that of Glenn Tinder when he advocated for an "attentive society," a place where people "listen seriously to those with whom they fundamentally disagree." Such a place would "provide room for strong convictions, but its defining characteristic would be a widespread willingness to give and receive assistance on the road to truth."[16] What Carter has advocated and what Tinder deems necessary goes far beyond toleration of religious views in the marketplace. It calls for, at a minimum, respect for religious viewpoints.

Conservative Christians have not lost the right to be heard because of past blunders or stoic silence during crucial times in our country's history. As Ralph Reed, executive director of the Christian Coalition, has said, "The 1960s and 1970s were decades in which faith and religious institutions lost much of their influence, and in which government policy became biased against the valuable social role religion plays in stabilizing marriages, nurturing young people, and knitting together communities."[17] Carter wants to see that influence restored. He does not want to see faith in God treated simply as a hobby. Carter writes, "We often seem most comfortable with people whose religion consists of nothing but a few private sessions of worship and prayer, but who are too secularized to let their faith influence the rest of the week."[18] Carter recognizes that for many Christians, religious beliefs directly impact the way in which they think, act, and live.

The Culture of Disbelief is not really about Christians or non-Christians, conservatives or liberals. It is neither a theological book nor simply a political one. Rather, *The Culture of Disbelief* is a book of reflection. Although legitimate criticism will be discussed, I have no doubt that the underlying premises Carter raises should cause all of us to reexamine our own view on religion and public life.

If I had only to write a few words which would sum up the thesis of *The Culture of Disbelief,* I would use the words of Supreme Court Justice William Brennan expressed in *McDaniel v. Paty:* "The Establishment Clause does not license government to treat religion and those who teach or practice it, simply by virtue of their status as such, as subversive of American ideals and therefore subject to unique disabilities."[19] Stephen Carter has done much to bring about a legitimate role for religion and religious perspective as they seek to address the issues of the day. Carter has recognized a truth which Irving Kristol had previously written, "religious conservatives are already too numerous to be shunted aside, and their numbers are growing, as is their

The Fight for Religious Liberty

influence. They are going to be the very core of an emerging American conservatism."

America, at this point in our history, has no choice but to respect the views of its religious citizens.

PART II. *Legitimate Criticism - Respect Is One Thing, Anticipation Is Another.*

Carter has acknowledged criticism which has been leveled at *The Culture of Disbelief.* In the foreword of the paperback edition Carter writes,

A handful of critics on the right have been disdainful of my own religion, all but calling me a bad Christian, evidently angry because of my support for ordination of women and for protecting gays and lesbians against discrimination in employment, as well as for what I describe in the book as my moderate pro-choice position. Not to be outdone, some on the left have objected to my treating as seriously the positions of conservative Christians with whom they disagree, the thesis of these critics evidently being that we will do well to exclude conservatives from the public square.[20]

Indeed, Michael Kinsley, in *The New Republic,* sharply criticized Carter for lacking any sense of the proportion of the problem and for confusing strong disagreement with intellectual bias.[21]

The thesis of religious views being trivialized is not what has drawn the rational criticism of conservatives. Rather, it is the apparent lack of conviction and inconsistencies in Carter's arguments. Richard Land, president of the Southern Baptist Christian Life Commission, has expressed concern about Carter's "maximum toleration" approach. Simple respect at the table of public policy is not enough; Land properly demands more. "What we want is maximum *acceptance,* maximum *acknowledgement,* maximum *accommodation,* because our duties and responsibilities to God as we understand them are far too important to allow any mere secular government to impose upon them"[22] (emphasis mine).

Land's criticism of Carter's "respect/maximum tolerance" concept does not go far enough. I propose that as our concepts and ideas are rationally based, eloquently stated, and at least reflective of those who may not agree with us, our input will be met with "anticipation." When our arguments, based upon our religious convictions, have the force of logic, one would hope that at the table of public policy our views would be looked at with

Christians in the Public Square

eager anticipation. This does not mean that everyone will always agree with us, but that our views will be deemed legitimate. George Weigel, I believe, would concur with my "anticipation" goal. Weigel writes, "The free and public exercise of religious conviction is not to be tolerated—it is to be accepted, welcomed, indeed, celebrated as the first of freedoms and the foundation of any meaningful scheme of human rights."[23]

Aside from the disagreement over what level of impact we should settle for, Carter himself has fallen into a trap which he cautioned his readers against. A trap which, in the paperback edition, he all but acknowledged as he explains some "changes" from the hardcover edition. Phillip E. Johnson, professor of law at the University of California, Berkeley, in reviewing *The Culture of Disbelief,* makes reference to what he calls "The Swedish Syndrome."[24] He writes, "Peter Berger once commented that if India is the most religious country in the world, and Sweden the least religious, then America is a nation of Indians ruled by Swedes."[25] Johnson, in a sense, underscores Carter's thesis when he draws out the Swedish Syndrome further, "From the Swedish viewpoint, the proposition that some supernatural being intervenes in the nature of human affairs, or reveals its will through 'Holy Scripture,' is inherently nonfactual."[26] But for Johnson, Carter's "respect" for religious views is not enough. Johnson accuses Carter of being a Swede in at least one aspect of his book. "For the most part, Carter simply urges the Swedes to treat the Indians with respect.... Treating people kindly is not the same thing as taking them seriously, however. When we take people seriously we grapple with their arguments, and consider the possibility that what they believe might actually be true."[27]

At first read, it would appear that Carter would accept Johnson's position. However, Johnson calls Carter on the carpet for his use of pejorative terms.

> What Carter calls the "religious right" in American politics represents a real challenge to Swedish power, and when he turns to this subject Carter loyally employs all the buzzwords of Swedish propaganda to crush the rebels. His chapter on the efforts of the Christian Coalition to elect candidates to local school boards is titled "Religious Fascism," although he says nothing about the group that remotely justifies the use of that ugly word.[28]

Apparently, Professor Carter has been influenced by Professor Johnson. In the paperback edition, Carter discusses the reasons

The Fight for Religious Liberty

why he changed the title of Chapter 13 from "Religious Fascism" to "Religious Future." Most notably, Carter explains what prompted the title change:

> Some readers formed the impression that because I discuss some in the conservative evangelical movement, and the Christian Coalition in particular, in Chapter 13, I must be referring to those movements as fascist. Although I have certainly had my differences with what has come to be known as the religious right, it was certainly not my intention to use so vicious and trite a label. I believe quite strongly in what I wrote in that Chapter: it is important not to be "McCarthyite about the Christian right." Too many commentators in the media, in politics, and in the academy make a casual habit of insulting their religious opponents instead of debating with them; I apologize to any reader who supposed that I was doing the same.[29]

The fact that Carter respectfully offered an apology is a sign that religious viewpoints are being more than tolerated or accommodated. They are being anticipated with thoughtful responses. Professor Johnson's just criticism was met with a just correction.

PART III: *From Anticipation to Engagement—What Shall We Then Do?*

As Paul Weyrich, president of Free Congress Foundation, has recognized, "As long as cultural deterioration continues to manifest itself in horrible ways, evangelicals will be compelled to get active."[30] As Christians, we engage the culture and seek relative peace. We must be mindful that politics is not the cure-all of moral decay. By involving ourselves in the political system, we are, in a sense, as Martin Luther said, "only patching and darning a culture that is unraveling." We involve ourselves in the battle to restrain evil out of love. Because we are commanded to "love our neighbors" (Lev. 19:18; Matt. 5:43), we must seek justice, care for creation, and make sure that evil principalities are not left unchecked.

"The Christian gospel tells us to be responsible and concerned citizens."[31] To be effective agents for change, we must be "in a continual process of understanding the present time" (Rom. 13:11).[32] As Gene Edward Veith, Jr. writes in *Postmodern Times,*

> The Church has always had to confront its culture and to exist in tension with the world. To ignore the

Christians in the Public Square

culture is to risk irrelevance; to accept the culture uncritically is to risk syncretism and unfaithfulness.... Orthodox Christians have also lived in every age, confessing their faith in Jesus Christ. They were part of the culture. Yet they also countered their culture, proclaiming God's law and gospel to society's very inadequacies and points of need.[33]

While we confront the culture, we must recognize that it is the gospel that transcends all political thought and influence. As Dutch theologian H.M. Kuiter has said, "The dead are not raised by politics."

Recognizing that our citizenship is not of this world does not relieve us of political involvement. As we engage the culture, we should pay attention to the words of the prophet Jeremiah: *"Seek the peace of the city where I have caused you to be carried away captive, and pray to the Lord for it; for in its peace you will have peace"* (Jer. 29:7) (emphasis mine). The word "seek" in Hebrew (*masa*) is not passive. It is an aggressive word meaning find after seeking, coming upon, or obtaining.[34] We, too, should seek justice through our political involvement. At the same time, we must, as the body of Christ, practice what we preach. Ron Sider, director of Evangelicals for Social Action, cautions all of us when he writes, "It is a farce for the church to ask Washington to legislate what Christians refuse to live."[35] Interestingly, it is Edward Dobson, former special assistant to Jerry Falwell, although on the opposite end of the political spectrum from Sider, who clearly supports his view. Dobson states "that we have no right to call for justice unless we ourselves are just in dealing with others."[36]

The question is how shall we as Christians live in the public square? We are to be the salt of the earth (preservative) and light of the world (exposing darkness) as Jesus commands (Matt. 5:13-16). In order to be salt and light, we must take several concrete steps. Politics means making hard decisions in real life situations. The following concepts, I believe, sum up our manner of engagement. They are not presented in order of importance.

First, we are required to *engage the culture*. We cannot lead monastic lives as the culture unravels around us. Secondly, we must *confront the issues* with rational, concrete proposals that will help our fellow citizens. Third, we must *point to the debris* that has been left in the wake of social policies which have failed. If we want our voice at the table anticipated, we need to utilize natural law, speak in an understandable grammar, and use empirical data whenever possible. We can do all of these things and remain

The Fight for Religious Liberty

distinctively Christian. Fourth, we must *love all people*. All of us have been created as images of God. We must treat all of God's images with dignity. Our love of neighbor is what should motivate us to political action. Fifth, through acts of mercy, we must seek to *heal the wounded*. Our policies on political issues involve real people with real problems, and we need to offer real solutions. Sixth, each of us in the spheres in which we find ourselves must *preach the gospel*. It is the message of the gospel which is the ultimate concern for all mankind. We should never concentrate so much on the temporal that we lose perspective of the eternal. What a tragedy it would be to change our laws without impacting the heart. Seventh, we must *live in hope*. Our hope is found in Jesus Christ. We should never place "political agendas on the same level or even in place of the more important message of the gospel itself."[37] The gospel is our ultimate hope, for it is the ultimate truth. Finally, our eighth concept is to *await Jesus' victorious return*. As we work for justice on earth, we should find our joy and solace, not in changed laws and policies—although they are important—but rather, it is the return of our Lord that motivates us to action.

What policies should we then seek on our road to relative peace? Richard John Neuhaus asked that we strive "to build a world in which the strong are just, and power is tempered by mercy, in which the weak are nurtured and the marginal embraced, and those at the entrance gates and those at the exit gates of life are protected both by law and love."[38] The prophet Micah recorded the words of the Lord reflecting similar thoughts, "He has shown you, O man, what is good; and what does the Lord require of you but to do justly, to love mercy, and to walk humbly with your God?" (Mic. 6:8).

Endnotes

[1] Stephen L. Carter, *The Culture of Disbelief: How American Law and Politics Trivialize Religious Devotion* (New York: Basic Books, 1993). I have also utilized the paperback edition of *The Culture of Disbelief* and have pointed to some significant changes Carter has made in the later edition.

[2] Richard John Neuhaus, *First Things*, 38 (December 1993), 68.

[3] Carter, 6.

[4] Carter, 10.

[5] *The Culture of Disbelief* (paperback edition: New York: Anchor Books, 1994), xvi.

Christians in the Public Square

[6]*Lamb's Chapel v. Center Moriches Union Free School District*, 113 S.Ct. 2141(1993). The author of this paper served as counsel of record in *Lamb's Chapel*.

[7]Brief for Respondent Attorney General, 24, *Lamb's Chapel* (No. 91-2024).

[8]Official Transcript, Proceeding Before The Supreme Court of the United States, 53-54.

[9]George Weigel, "Talking the Talk: Christian Conviction and Democratic Etiquette" in *Disciples and Democracy: Religious Conservatives and the Future of American Politics,* edited by Michael Cromartie (Grand Rapids: Eerdmans Publishing, 1994), 83.

[10]Fred Barnes, "Why the Nation Needs the Religious Right," *Disciples and Democracy,* edited by Michael Cromartie, 114.

[11]Carter, *The Culture of Disbelief,* (Dedication Page).

[12]Michael Horowitz, "What Religious Conservatives Want," *Disciples and Democracy,* edited by Michael Cromartie, 21.

[13]Carter, *The Culture of Disbelief,* 38.

[14]*Religion and American Politics: From the Colonial Period to the 1980s,* ed. Mark A. Noll (New York: Oxford University Press, 1990).

[15]James W. Skillen, *The Scattered Voice. Christians at Odds in the Public Square* (Regent College 1990), Chapter 6, "Civil Rights Reformers," 119.

[16]Glenn Tinder, "The Spirit of Freedom: To Live Attentively," in Richard John Neuhaus and George Weigel, eds., *Being Christian Today: An American Conversation* (Washington D.C.: Ethics and Public Policy Center, 1992), 152-53.

[17]Ralph Reed, "What Conservatives Want," *Disciples and Democracy,* ed. by Michael Cromartie, 6.

[18]Carter, *The Culture of Disbelief,* 29.

[19]*McDaniel v. Paty,* 435 U.A. 618, 640 (1978) (Brennan, J. concurring).

[20]"Taking Religious Conservatives Seriously," *Disciples and Democracy,* ed. Michael Cromartie, viii.

[21]Michael Kinsley, "The Culture of Disbelief," *The New Republic,* September 13, 1993.

[22]Richard Land, "Talking the Talk," (Response), *Disciples and Democracy,* ed. Michael Cromartie, 101.

[23]George Weigel, "Talking the Talk," *Disciples and Democracy,* ed. Michael Cromartie, 91 .

[24]Phillip E. Johnson, *First Things* 38 (December 1993), "The Swedish Syndrome," 48.

[25]Ibid.

The Fight for Religious Liberty

[26]Ibid.
[27]Ibid., 48-49.
[28]Ibid., 49.
[29]*The Culture of Disbelief* (paperback edition 1994), xx.
[30]*No Longer Exiles,* "The Religious Right: A Historical Overview," ed. Michael Cromartie, comment by Paul Weyrich, 26.
[31]Michael Cromartie, "Up to Our Steeples in Politics," 59.
[32]Gene Edward Veith, Jr., *Postmodern Times: A Christian Guide to Contemporary Thought and Culture* (Westchester, Ill.: Crossway Books, 1994), xii.
[33]Ibid.
[34]*The New International Dictionary of New Testament Theology,* Vol. 3, 527-28.
[35]Skillen, *The Scattered Voice,* 143.
[36]Edward Dobson, *The Bible, Politics and Democracy* (Grand Rapids: Eerdmans Publishing, 1987), 11.
[37]Michael Cromartie, "Up to Our Steeples in Politics," 58.
[38]Ibid., 53.

BEING SALT IN AN UNSAVORY WORLD
The Spiritual Cancer of Pornography and How to Fight It

By Dee A. Jepsen

I want to share with you, first, as a believer—a follower of Jesus Christ; secondly, as president of "Enough is Enough!", a nonprofit organization combating illegal pornography; and, just as importantly, as a citizen and as a woman. My topic is an unpleasant one, to say the least, and perhaps it seems somewhat unusual for a woman to be addressing the issue of pornography. I actually believe it is very appropriate for a woman to be addressing this issue of pornography, because we women are its primary subjects and its primary victims—we and our children. Women, therefore, can speak with a special authority about pornography.

I am going to share some information about the cancerous pornography that is eating away at the tissue of society, and how each of us can be a part of stopping its growth. But let's take a brief look first at why all of us who are members of the body of Christ should get involved in the battle against pornography. This really speaks to a larger issue. Should Christians be involved in the debate and the activities in the public square? We hear much today about the cultural war. And there surely is one being waged. But should this be our battle, as followers of Jesus, the Prince of Peace?

Christians in the Public Square

Jesus admonished us to be the salt of the earth and the light of the world. How can we, the body of Christ, be the salt of the earth if we never get out of the shaker? How can we be the light of the world if we never get out from under the bushel? The loss of America's moral compass—a public square that is stripped of the recognition of intrinsic values—is due to the fact that for many years the salt was kept in the shaker and the light was kept under the bushel.

The term "separation of church and state" has been used by many to keep Christians out of the public square, away from our rightful responsibility to help direct the course of public affairs. Other voices have filled the vacuum left by the absence of our voices, and the latest public opinion polls now establish contemporary morality. And our nation, our people, and especially our children, are suffering for that.

As I am sure you know, our founders never intended for this to happen to America. They gave us a nation, flawed by its own humanity, yet aspiring to exist as a society in which free men and women could live under God, by His laws, in their individual and corporate lives, as these laws were applied through civil government. True history abounds with evidence of the nature of their noble endeavor. Here are just a couple of quotes attesting to their purposes and beliefs.

George Washington: "It is impossible to govern the world without God and the Bible."

James Madison: "We have staked the whole future of American civilization, not upon the power of government, far from it. We have staked the future of all of our political institutions...upon the capacity of each and all of us to govern ourselves, to control ourselves, to sustain ourselves according to the Ten Commandments of God."

John Adams: "Statesmen...may plan and speculate for liberty, but it is religion and morality alone which can establish the principles upon which freedom can securely stand. The only foundation of a free constitution is pure virtue."

Many deny our nation's Christian roots, but research into original historical documents and letters, both public and private, defy the "revisionist history" that is all too often spouted today.

The syndicated columnist Joseph Sobran recently stated, somewhat cynically, "The unhappy truth is that America is being hen-pecked by a class of half-educated people—people who have been to college and are exposed too much, and too exclusively, to others of the same breed; hip, clever, shallow, and collectively all too sure of themselves."

Being Salt in an Unsavory World

Many who criticize Christians and their belief in moral absolutes, decrying Christian involvement in the political process, have based their views upon misinformation and a lack of knowledge and understanding.

Today tolerance is celebrated as the chief of virtues, but I would submit to you that there are some things that are *intolerable*. Today we also are urged to "accept," in a public context, lifestyles and behaviors that many Americans, and especially those who are Bible-believing Christians, believe to be morally wrong and personally and culturally destructive. Again I would submit that there are some things that are simply *unacceptable*. As Christians we know that "people" must be loved, not judged, but lifestyles and actions are to be judged. It is not compassion to condone sin, when the wages of sin is death. We need to remember the old admonition about hating the sin, but loving the sinner. There are times, however, when it is only by God's grace that we can do that.

Today "choice" is presented of greatest value. As individual "rights" are touted as supreme, we seem, as a culture, to forget that there are some choices that are clearly wrong and destructive, and that rights carry with them certain responsibilities.

We all realize that we have moral and social problems in our country today, but the good news is that a new awareness of America's moral crisis is growing across the country. The public has become aware that we have a problem. Quite simply, the by-products of throwing out God's Law—stripping His moral absolutes from our lives and culture—are chaos and destruction. Because contemporary culture is fraught with problems on every hand, there is a new openness to returning to what is now being called "family values" or "traditional values." This is a day of great opportunity for Christians to give the leadership needed to bring our country back to its moral heritage.

Being a leader is not easy. It requires great dedication, the enduring of criticism, and often doing what you really don't want to do. But we all have an opportunity to leave an imprint of goodness on our portion of history, to leave an inheritance for our children and grandchildren that is beyond the material, a moral inheritance and a culture that reflects God's standards. If we choose not to pay the price to give that kind of leadership, our children will suffer the consequences and the future they will inherit will be diminished.

One of the moral issues that we believers must address is the very distasteful subject of pornography. I'm going to share some information you probably would just as soon not hear, not just

Christians in the Public Square

because it is unpleasant, but once you know the magnitude of the problem of pornography and the way it affects our culture and could affect those you love, you will have to make a choice. Either you will give some form of leadership to help solve the problem, or you will do nothing and will feel guilty. You will bear the responsibility of "knowing" about the problem.

If anyone had told me ten years ago that I would be working full-time in the battle against pornography, I would not have believed them, nor would I have been very happy about the prospect. But women speak with a special authority on the issue of pornography, and it is crucial that they be involved in addressing this cultural problem. That is why the "Enough is Enough!" campaign against pornography is directed by women, even though we have numerous men involved with us, and that is why we have placed a special focused effort to involve women and to have them take some ownership in solving this problem.

We women have a special stake in the issue because of its effect, not only upon our own lives—as women it degrades and demeans us—but we are concerned about pornography's effect upon our children—it victimizes them. We are also concerned about pornography's effect upon our husbands and our marriages—it can ruin them—and we are concerned about pornography's effect upon our national culture.

Please indulge me now as I put in a "plug" for women and their influence in society and highlight why you should encourage their involvement. I often remind women that they are more than half our population, they generally vote in greater numbers than men, and they transact the majority of retail sales. And when they are Christian women, they are powerful prayer warriors. That combination means clout, no matter how you look at it. I encourage women to use their individual and corporate influence to change the moral direction of the nation. This in no way is meant to slight the influence and moral obligations of men, but rather to encourage women, who often do not "know" their own ability to influence. In today's world we women know we can learn, produce, and earn, but often we do not give much thought to our ability to influence the moral course of our culture, and our responsibility to do so.

The "mother-heart" of love, which I believe is a divine gift to womankind—the mothers of the world—has a special capacity to love and to reach out in compassion. Those women who are members of the community of faith also share a spiritual motivation, which is one of the strongest of all motivations. Where pornography is concerned, women of faith need to be challenged to

Being Salt in an Unsavory World

pray, to stand up, to speak out, and then to act on behalf of their own dignity, the welfare of their children and marriages, and on behalf of the welfare of the society in which they live.

I came across a wonderful quote in *Democracy in America,* by the French historian, Alexis de Tocqueville, who came to America to try to identify what made this the unique and successful country it had already become. He then wrote this well-recognized book, setting forth his analysis of our country. I had often heard him quoted about the influence of the churches in America, but I found he also wrote of America's women. In Chapter 12 he states,

As for my part, I have no hesitation in saying that although the American woman never leaves her domestic sphere and is in some respects very dependent within it, nowhere does she enjoy a higher station. And now that I come near the end of this book in which I have recorded so many considerable achievements of the Americans, if anyone asks me what I think is the chief cause of the extraordinary prosperity and growing power of this nation, I should answer it is due to the superiority of their women.[1]

The author noted that though couples may have shared the same values, when the men got involved in the commerce of the day they often started to compromise, but the women stood firm. There is a tenacity in that mother-heart with which women are gifted that is a tenacity second to none, and you know that it manifests itself in the church as well.

It was to harness that tenacity in the battle against pornography that a woman named Sarah Blanken, the vice president for women's leadership in what is now called the National Coalition for the Protection of Children and Families, called together a group of thirty women in Washington, D.C., in February of 1990. They were leaders in various professions, denominations, and faiths. I was privileged to be among those women. Had we gotten off the topic of illegal pornography that day, we would have had strenuous disagreements. We did not. Susan Baker, whose husband was then Secretary of State, and Tipper Gore came to the meeting, due to their interest at the time in the labeling of rock music lyrics. Susan showed us some slides of the pornography that was available in the market of the day. We were appalled! I know now that the slides we viewed were mild, when compared to what even our children can view today with a computer and a modem.

From this meeting of thirty women developed the "Enough is Enough!" women's campaign against pornography, about which in

Christians in the Public Square

November of 1995 *The New York Times* wrote,

> Ms. Hughes and Ms. Jepsen (representatives of "Enough is Enough!") were instrumental in drumming up support for a bill (Computer Decency Act) that passed the Senate in June to impose jail terms and heavy penalties on people who knowingly transmit material that is deemed "obscene, lewd, lascivious, filthy or indecent."...
> "Their mediating role has been a key one," said Senator Jim Exon, Democrat of Nebraska and sponsor of the bill.

The campaign was publicly launched three and a half years ago at a press conference at the National Press Club. We faced that day a room packed with secular journalists. We showed them a few select slides, with blacked out areas, at the outset of the meeting, telling them that they needed to know what kind of material we were going to be talking about. We referenced the diversity of the founding group of women, then at the close of the meeting they heard from a young mother named Diane.

The mother, Diane, told how her three-year-old little girl—her "baby"—had been raped and sexually violated in every way imaginable by a twelve-year-old neighbor boy. The boy was from a good, intact home and had never been in trouble. The police felt sure they would find he had been sexually abused. That was not the case. After a thorough psycho-sexual evaluation they found there was only one motivating factor involved in his heinous actions. He was imitating pornography he had gotten at a summer youth camp, where his parents had sent him to enrich his life.

As that shattered mother spoke, experienced, hardened newsmen listened with tears in their eyes. Everyone present was vividly reminded that victims are real people. There were no hostile questions. We had no damage control to handle, and we have to this day been blessed with good media.

We chose the name "Enough is Enough!" for our campaign because it speaks the sentiments of so many. We had watched pornography and all its deadly effects upon individual and corporate life taking its toll before our eyes, and yet not enough had been done about it. There had been some efforts, surely, yet to the general public, pornography and its harms had not been a priority issue. "Enough is Enough!" joined the battle to change that, to move the issue of pornography to its rightful place—as a priority item when addressing the public health and safety agenda of our society, and, for those of us who share a religious faith, among the top items to be addressed as we confront moral decadence.

Being Salt in an Unsavory World

This material is not only destructive to individual lives, those made in the image of God, for whom Jesus died; it is also an offense to the righteousness of God and His holiness. The church of Jesus Christ can do no less than stand against and rout out the moral cancer of pornography. If it does not, I believe it will stand in judgment for that inaction.

As a matter of policy, "Enough is Enough!" focuses upon pornography that is "illegal." We seek to educate, equip, and mobilize citizens on the issue of pornography. When the word "pornography" is spoken most Americans think of airbrushed nudity—*Playboy*, etc. Many do not realize the illegal, depraved kind of pornographic material easily available today. *Playboy* and publications of that nature are considered legal material for adults, even though you and I may see them as having a very destructive effect, and likely to lead into the use of more graphic and violent material—much like marijuana serves as a gateway drug into harder drugs. Nonetheless, this material is legal for adults.

There is now much misinformation about pornography, and I will attempt to clarify some of it here. There is a great deal of discussion in the public debate about what is called "the freedom of speech" issue where pornography is concerned. Since pornography is a large, money-making industry primarily controlled by organized crime, an industry that produces 8 to 10 billion dollars a year in profit, there is great opposition to anything which would dry up this profiteering business. The pornographers involved in this lucrative industry and their very highly paid attorneys have done a good job creating a smoke screen of confusion about pornography: what it is, how available it is—even to children—its harm to individuals and to our culture, and the fact that much of it is illegal.

The Supreme Court has said that certain types of pornography are not protected speech, just like slander, libel, and false advertising are not protected speech. Dealing with this type of material, then, is not a First Amendment violation. We need to understand that and not be intimidated into silence or inaction on the matter by First Amendment extremists.

The types of pornography that are illegal are as follows:
- child pornography (pictures of a crime scene in progress—a child being sexually molested);
- obscenity (hard-core pornography);
- material that is harmful to minors (soft-core pornography that is considered legal for adults is illegal when available to minors);

Christians in the Public Square

- broadcast indecency—the Federal Communications Commission (FCC) is the arbiter where this material is concerned.

Most women, and many men, regardless of their political inclinations or religious (or nonreligious) beliefs, oppose illegal pornography and its adverse effects; therefore, our campaign strategy was to join together in a unique coalition all those women, and supportive men, who object to illegal pornography's invasion of our common culture. To this point, that has proven to be a valid and effective strategy.

Another great untruth spread about the effects of pornography is that pornography is not harmful; it doesn't have any victims. That is a lie. Anyone who counsels hurting people knows that is a lie.

As one who has looked into the eyes and hearts of hundreds of victims of pornography's prey—women and children, and sometimes addicted men—no one can tell me that pornography has no victims. No one can tell that to the middle-aged woman who recently slipped a note to me after I had spoken on this issue saying, "Thank you for what you are doing to battle pornography. I am one of its victims. Pornography amputated my self-esteem at the age of eight." And she has borne the scar of that assault on her personhood every day of every year since that time. She's one of millions.

Sexual abuse at any age is devastating. But sexual abuse, even just fondling, at a young age has an absolutely devastating effect upon children. It is an invasion of their very personhood, a degrading, humiliating experience. I do not totally understand why this has such a great impact, but in some mysterious way our very identity is tied to our sexuality. The first thing that is said when we enter this world at birth is, "It's a boy!" or "It's a girl!" Somehow we and our very worth are deeply violated when we are sexually abused.

The proponents of pornography say, "Well, all of these harms of pornography you talk about are only 'anecdotal'. These are only based upon incidences—stories of human experience. There is no scientific proof of pornography's harm."

To those defenders of pornography who cite lack of "scientific" proof, I would say, "It's true you cannot put the motivations of the human heart in a test tube and prove their validity. If you cannot prove that pornography negatively affects human behavior, then neither can you 'prove' the existence of love. But tell me that love doesn't exist!" Of course, love does exist, and of course, there are harms from pornography!

What are the harms of pornography? Let me just quickly list

Being Salt in an Unsavory World

categories of these harms. There are numerous studies available that attest to these harms.

1. Pornography plays a major role in the molestation of children. It is used to stimulate the perpetrator, lower the inhibitions of the children, and as an instruction manual to show them what to do. More than 80 percent of convicted child molesters admit to the regular use of hard-core pornography, and most often in the commission of their crimes (W. Marshall, "Report on the Use of Pornography by Sexual Offenders," Report to the Federal Department of Justice, Ottawa, Canada, 1983). The most popular pornography video series in America is based on incest, and it sometimes is available in local Mom-and-Pop video stores.

2. It encourages rape and the rape myth (that when a woman says "no" she means "yes," and she likes violence). Rape in the U.S. has risen 500 percent since 1960. The National Victims Center reports that at least one woman is raped every 46 seconds, and 29 percent of all forcible rapes occur on victims 11 years old or younger. Another study by Dr. W. Marshall found that 86 percent of convicted rapists admitted to the regular use of pornography.

3. It is addictive to many men, an escalating addiction that many times ends in acts of sexual violence. Some counseling professionals believe that addiction to pornography is more difficult to overcome than addiction to drugs and alcohol. Studies by Dr. Victor Cline of the University of Utah show a step-by-step progression among many who consume pornography:
   (1) Addiction
   (2) Escalation
   (3) Desensitization
   (4) Acting Out

Acting out often leads to acts of sexual and domestic violence as well as spousal and child abuse.

4. It encourages behavior that contributes to the transmission of sexually transmitted diseases.

5. It negatively affects attitudes and values. (It eroticizes inequality and violence and gives permission to treat women and children in a degrading, debasing manner.)

This material leads men to have unrealistic expectations of their spouses. What woman can live up to being compared to airbrushed photographs of young and beautiful models, especially as the natural process of aging takes place? Some say that married couples can enhance their sexual relationship with their spouse by using pornography. Dr. Barbara DeAngelis, well-known professional counselor dealing with relationships, says that using this material interjects a third element into a marriage and is

Christians in the Public Square

destructive. She adds that what some see as intimacy, in this case is really eroticism. Eroticism will not last, and may destroy intimacy.

Our goal is to change the way America thinks about pornography, much the way in which Mothers Against Drunk Driving (MADD) changed the way America thinks about drinking and driving. Not only did MADD in ten years change laws about drinking and driving, and prompted the aggressive enforcement of those laws, attitudes about drinking to excess changed as well. I believe as Americans become educated about the harms of illegal pornography their attitudes about the use of illegal pornography will be changed as well. Due to the recent media focus upon "cyberporn," pornography has been thrust into prominence on America's reassessment agenda. Our organization's efforts toward making this problem a priority item and focusing America's attention upon it were assisted and accelerated by computer porn. The problem of pornography is an issue whose time has come.

Recently, "Prime Time" did a television program on children and sex, starkly revealing that children ten and younger are being "sexualized" due to constant exposure to sexually oriented materials. As our common culture has become coarser, children have been robbed of their childhood. A time of innocence has been stolen away from today's children. It is time that adults of this nation take responsibility to combat the predators who are polluting the minds of our nation's most valuable resource—our children. Moms and dads, grandmothers and grandfathers—all responsible citizens—must not accept the feeble defense that there is nothing we can do to protect the well-being and safety of children.

Clinical studies and life experiences attest to the fact that pornography numbs the moral conscience, stunts moral growth, and encourages anti-social behavior. In our work with victims, we continually look into the eyes and hear the hearts of those who have been bruised and broken by the effects of pornography. When we allow pornography to be freely available to children, pornography is not only an attack upon the present, but an attack upon the future as well. Once pornography has been viewed by young, vulnerable children, it can start a chain of abuse that carries over into their adult and family lives. You cannot simply push the delete button and eliminate those pornographic images from their memories; they will continue to play over and over again in the theater of their minds—perhaps for life.

Children exposed at an impressionable age to this material can have their attitudes and behaviors warped and their view of

Being Salt in an Unsavory World

human dignity and sexuality distorted. Last year this story was picked up by the Associated Press:

Across Florida, thousands of children rape and molest other children, the state has found since it began gathering information last year. In 1,548 reports collected in the first six months, nearly half the victims were younger than five. Researchers say most young sex offenders have been physically or sexually abused and many have been exposed to violence or pornography at an early age.

The Washington Times ran a story with this quote on February 26, 1996: "The ten-year-old boy told the judge that, after watching a (scrambled) sex-cable channel, he decided to experiment. He then proceeded to rape a five-year-old-girl." This is just one of many cases.

Here's one from Maryland, that appeared in a Washington paper.

Prince George's County police charged a ten-year-old Suitland boy with raping a four-year-old girl Wednesday, but they couldn't charge his accomplice because he was too young—six years old.... William Garrison, chairman of the psychology department at Children's Hospital, said, 'The boys may have been influenced by television or sexual acts they have witnessed.' A similar incident occurred in Isle of Wight, Va., where a ten-year-old boy, charged with raping and sodomizing a six-year-old girl, confessed he was imitating what he saw in a video, police said.

A Southern California newspaper reported: "We're finding kids younger and younger committing acts of considerable violence," said Jill Ferrell, director of Safer Society Resources of Michigan.

"The first step is getting families and communities to acknowledge that children can sexually abuse other children," notes Carolyn Cunningham, clinic director of Cedar House, a Long Beach center for the treatment of abused and neglected children and their families. "But there is a difference between young children comparing their anatomies and 'coercive sex abuse,'" she said. "We don't want to label these children as rapists, but the issue is just that serious."

Over the years the pornography industry has had two basic business goals: to remove as much of the social stigma as possible from consuming pornography; and to use every advance in

Christians in the Public Square

technology to lessen the difficulty of purchasing and consuming pornography.

Until the late 1970s, pornography was primarily available in magazines and 8mm film loops, usually in the "bad part of town."

In the 1980s the VCR was exploited by pornographers. Consumers could purchase videos and watch pornography right in their own homes. Satellite technology and cable television led to further inroads by pornographers worldwide.

Then came personal computers (PCs), and a whole new world of pornography access rushed in through its floodgate. Computer-related developments will shape how the pornography industry seeks to market its products over the next quarter-century. And who will suffer the most? The children!

Today, we face an insidious threat—hard-core pornography, child pornography, and "indecent" material which is harmful to minors are being transmitted over the Internet directly into our homes. The Information Super Highway has been invaded by morally irresponsible, reckless drivers, who travel the Highway with total disregard for the damage inflicted on young minds through the pornography they provide. Children are usually more adept than adults at operating computers, and today, with little effort, a child with a computer and a modem can download the most vile and perverse, often violent, hard-core pornography ever produced. This material includes such themes as incest, rape, bestiality (actual sex with most of the animals in Noah's Ark), torture, and mutilation. This material can be accessed in full and clear color with just a few computer key clicks. This is pornography that the Supreme Court has ruled not to be protected speech and is illegal for adults as well as children.

The recently passed Telecommunications Act included a section, the Communications Decency Act, that addresses computer pornography. "Enough is Enough!" has been acknowledged as playing a major role in its passage, by moving the debate from one on technology alone to one involving the protection of children. This legislation applied existing laws regarding pornography to the new computer technology. This section of the Telecommunications Act is now being challenged in court by the ACLU and others, but we are hopeful that the challenge will be overturned.

The focus of the objections to the law is the outlawing of "indecent" material for children—material legal for adults, but not for children. This material is not protected speech and is already legislated against in most states and many local communities under the rubric of "material harmful to minors." With the advent

Being Salt in an Unsavory World

of computers which send hard-core pornography and indecent material across state lines, this federal legislation was needed. Its passage was an enormous victory in the battle against pornography, and was supported on a bipartisan basis.

The ACLU and their cohorts, in objecting to this recent legislation, insist it is the parents' sole responsibility to protect the children from pornography on the Internet. This argument entirely shifts the baseline. Prior to this technology you had to seek out and pay for pornography. Opponents are suggesting the entire answer is for parents to invest their time and spend their money to pay for software to keep pornography away from their children. This is a paradigm shift in approach.

"Enough is Enough!" believes parents should be involved; however, we hold the view that it will take three components to effectively address the computer pornography issue and its access to children, as follows:

- effective laws and aggressive law enforcement;
- educated parents who monitor their children's computer use; and
- a technology industry working to address the problem through technology.

We are pleased that many in the industry are developing filtering systems so parents can block some material and monitor their children's on-line activity. There are a number of good filtering software packages available today. "Enough is Enough!" believes one of the best is Rated PG, and we are grateful that a portion of the sales price is being contributed to the educational work of our organization. This is an important tool for parents, since not only is computer pornography a problem, but the Internet is the new playground the pedophiles—those with a sexual appetite for children—prowl looking for their young prey.

For many this is a difficult issue, since pornography holds a fatal attraction to many men, and they are uncomfortable addressing this material. Women, on the other hand, have found this issue a challenge because it is so distasteful. But address this issue we must—women and men—or our children and our grandchildren will pay the price for our negligence. This problem is in the church, just as in every other segment of society. It is in the pews, and unfortunately, sometimes in the pulpit. We must face this dirty task and get involved. I encourage you to do so in your church. We have many materials and strategies available for your use.

Pornography invades the thoughts and manipulates behavior; it produces bondage. It erodes the character of individuals and nations; it seduces self-control and self-government, and,

Christians in the Public Square

therefore, demolishes the very foundation of adherence to law—both divine and civic. It is toxic. It must be opposed.

And as we oppose it, let us speak the truth in love, as we are admonished to do in God's Word. As we seek to be salt in an unsavory world, let us not judge, but love. Remember, we have a Savior—the Creator of all things—Who went to the cross and died for us. The sinless Savior—perfect in all ways—still stood as a lamb before the slaughterer. He did not defend or condemn; He loved and forgave even those who hung Him in humiliation. He never compromised righteousness, but He always loved. He always called "sin" "sin," but He always loved. He never touted Himself and His righteousness, but He always loved. Pray God we may be the same.

Endnotes

[1]Alexis de Tocqueville, *Democracy in America,* Vol. II, the Henry Reeve text as revised by Francis Bowen, (New York: Alfred A. Knopf) 1980, 214

THE CHRISTIAN, THE MEDIA, AND THE ISSUES

By Gary Ledbetter

Indiana has the third largest Amish population in the United States. When we lived there, we liked to visit among the neat farms and obviously different lifestyle of the northern Indiana Amish country. What was a little surprising was the realization that these folks were serious in their rejection of most twentieth century innovations. They regarded us as unwelcome gawkers as they went about their daily lives. We outsiders were "the English" to the Amish because of the language we spoke. We were the ones who subjected ourselves and our children to a godless culture; we were the outsiders chasing buggies or standing in Amish front lawns taking unwelcome pictures of a culture about which we had little understanding.

Evangelical Christians have a similar relationship with the secular media. To the media we are nineteenth-century men who reject reasonable social innovation. We are viewed as racist, homophobic, unenlightened, somber folks who fear the culture in which we live. To us, on the other hand, the media appear liberal, godless, shallow, and clueless about anything more eternal than today's opinion polls. These are stereotypes that do not stand up to scrutiny, but they do reflect the lack of understanding that exists between those who influence public opinion on so many crucial issues and we who believe we hold more thoughtful perspectives on those issues. This is a reason that when you or I get a call from a local newspaper or television station, we are tempted to refuse

Christians in the Public Square

the interview. There are also reasons why we should be ready and willing to talk to the press regarding the ways in which our faith instructs our understanding of timely issues.

Why Should They Talk to You?

News is a business, after all. People are more likely to buy papers or watch a broadcast that surprises, amuses, informs, or titillates them. If your views are quaint to a reporter, he assumes that people will at least be amused. It is not news to find that most mainstream church spokesmen think that capital punishment is barbaric and sub-Christian. A reporter is challenged to find an articulate person to take the other viewpoint—that the Bible does allow government to dispense the death penalty. I served this purpose for a news writer in Indianapolis who ended up quoting six religious professionals, only one of which accepted capital punishment as a legitimate expression of government power. It was my dissenting opinion that made the story interesting, although the weight of "reason and compassion" was on the other side. After a while a writer learns that there are any number of people who will stand up for the traditional social gospel; the valued contacts are those conservatives who are to any degree articulate and willing to be quoted.

To answer the question another way, reporters should talk to you because you are an informed opinion with a reputation for concern about public issues. If you write for a local Christian newspaper, speak or preach on the radio, do a good job of promoting your church or ministry, or if you participate in an issues-oriented group or project, you will eventually be called to comment about a relevant local issue. I was called by the daily paper in Indianapolis primarily for three reasons: The local religion writer read the *Indiana Baptist,* I worked for the state convention, and I was an officer in a state pro-life organization. In a smaller town, you may be the pastor of the largest Baptist church or the church with a food closet or the church that sponsors a life chain or the church that sponsored the anti-casino rally.

Why Should You Talk to Them?

Two things often go through our minds when we are called for a comment or interview. First, we might be flattered that anyone wants to hear what we have to say. Second, we may be fearful that the pagans will misquote or misuse what we say. Although being flattered can lead to the fulfillment of your worst fears, I would urge you to make yourself available when you are called upon. For one thing, your willingness to offer your biblical viewpoint will put you in the writer's Rolodex. ("This guy will talk to us from this per-

The Christian, the Media, and the Issues

spective, so let's remember to use him in the future.") Such contacts are valuable to the reporter and can sometime serve your own desired purposes if you are willing to stick your neck out a little.

Another reason you might want to grant the interview is for the sake of encouragement. Most Americans, to say nothing of most Christians, believe that homosexual behavior is destructive, capital punishment should be administered in some cases, and that abortion-on-demand is immoral. If the news media are to have any chance of acknowledging those viewpoints, someone has to be willing to be quoted. Even if the reporter himself believes these things, he is not supposed to quote himself; he must find a spokesman. It does mean something to those who read your quotes to see their own beliefs or your church's witness given some kind of prominence. I once sat on a three-hour radio panel with a live audience and call-in questions. The subject was civil rights legislation for homosexuals. The panel was made up of six professional homosexuals, one liberal moderator, and two Christian guys in ties. The audience was made up of fifty homosexuals and three friends of mine, who also were wearing ties. We looked like five Mormon missionaries in the wrong place. The three hours were miserable. I did not do well and, except for some great witnessing opportunities during the frequent breaks, it seemed like a total loss and an embarrassment. I changed my mind as I talked to laymen in my church who, though they would have been terrified to participate in such a forum, were very encouraged to hear someone speaking for them in such a place. I also heard of occasions where the program spawned witnessing opportunities in homes and workplaces where the radio was playing. It was not enjoyable, but I think it was worthwhile.

I agree with those who believe that post-Watergate journalism, religious and otherwise, is unworthy of the title. Many of you know of times when facts or perspectives have been seriously warped in the writer's haste to use the word "extreme" or "fundamentalist" to portray ideas or people we know to be merely Christian. At the level where our communities are influenced, however, the editor of the local newspaper is just a guy who is as likely to go to church or hate big government as the next guy. It is at this level that we have the chance to air our viewpoints and represent our faith with the greatest effectiveness. We who regularly stand before a crowd or radio audience in order to proclaim the gospel should be just as ready and willing to speak to those who have never heard biblical answers to the questions raised in the evening news.

Christians in the Public Square

Some Guidelines for Dealing with the Media

I have found the following dos and don'ts to be helpful when the media call concerning some public policy issues:

1. *Be aware of current events.* Folks who read the newspapers usually know what kinds of things the community is dealing with. If the state is about to put a local man to death for murder, you may be asked to comment on your viewpoints on this subject. You will have nothing to share if you do not know about the gambling initiative or the informed consent bill in the state house or whatever is happening that affects public policy.

2. *Be prepared.* There may be times when you are on the hot seat and have several opportunities to give interviews. A fact or note sheet will serve you well as you deal with the same information repeatedly. As a leader, you can assume someone will ask you about timely issues. A little preparation will allow you to answer appropriately, rather than dodge the questions put to you.

3. *Be concise.* Newspaper writers (and readers) are not very interested in the ante-Nicene fathers or in Southern Baptist polity. They also are not calling you just to chat. Think a few moments if you need to, but say what you have to say in a few, clear sentences. It is reasonable to ask if you can call the writer back in ten minutes if you need to collect your thoughts. Rambling on is fatal for a couple of reasons. First, you are hard to quote, and you may not be happy with what the writer targets as a quote. If you are concise, the quotes you give will be the ones used in some form or another. Second, if you wander aimlessly, you are much more likely to say something you did not intend to say. A good interviewer will allow an "awkward silence" in the hope that you will just keep talking until you say something provocative.

4. *Be sure of what you say.* A reporter is under no obligation to honor your request to keep a quote off the record after you have said it. Don't say things that should be off the record to anyone you do not trust—a lot. My wife, who has written several investigative pieces, would counsel that you don't say it to *anyone* if you don't want to be quoted. She has been given leads on many occasions through casual conversation. A fair writer will not quote dinner conversation, but it is impossible to not know something once you've heard it. Don't guess or generalize about things that are important.

5. *Be sensitive to the needs and interests of the person you are talking to.* The writer is also curious about you and your

The Christian, the Media, and the Issues

beliefs. Your courtesy and concern for the person you are talking to may meet spiritual needs in his life.

6. *Don't be too forthcoming.* If you answer questions that are not asked, you may open a can of worms you did not want to discuss.

7. *Don't try to change the discussion.* A question about a casino gambling referendum does not call for an answer about the evils of strong drink. You will be ignored or portrayed as a goof.

8. *Don't make personal attacks.* Let your arguments speak for you. You can be sure that someone who thinks you are wrong will be quoted. You may even know who the opposition spokesman will be. His character or his behavior is not really relevant. You could effectively address common arguments the opposition might be expected to use. Stick to the issues. The truth usually will win out; even if it doesn't, it should be what we are about.

9. *Don't speak for others.* You may be asked to speculate about another's opinion or response. Even if you can guess, avoid answering such questions. "I don't know," or "I wouldn't want to guess," or "You'll need to ask him that" can be an acceptable answer. Either the reporter is trying to trap you or he is being lazy. Be polite, but don't answer dumb questions.

10. *Don't say "no comment" unless you can't help it.* It is the equivalent of hanging up the phone. It makes you appear defensive or sinister or hostile.

11. *Don't assume a level of knowledge on the part of the interviewer.* It may be hard to balance this with the avoidance of being pedantic, but your church and denomination are hard enough for members to understand; imagine what it must be like for an outsider. Using the language of Zion, acronyms, or words specific to your church or group will only hinder your effort to get your point across. The same is true of unusual vocabulary words such as "pedantic."

Making a Significant Difference

HAVE YOU GOT GOOD RELIGION?

By Gary Frost

It's funny how we often listen without hearing. We take in great deals of information without really processing it.

This fact was brought home to me recently when my ten-year-old son was trying to quiet the fussy whimpering of my eight-month-old son. My ten-year-old began singing a very familiar song:

>Rockabye baby on the tree top,
>When the wind blows the cradle will rock.
>When the bough breaks the cradle will fall
>And down will come baby, cradle and all.

If we really hear the words of this favorite lullaby we discover that what it presents is not very comforting. I believe that too often God's people hear His Word as if it were a beautiful lullaby.

As Christ spoke to the churches in Asia Minor in the Book of Revelation, He said: "He that hath an ear let him hear what the Spirit saith unto the church."

I don't claim to be a modern-day mystic with unique and personal access to the Holy Spirit beyond that of other believers, but I do know that Isaiah 58 is a timely word that the Spirit is speaking to the people of God in this present age, and we would do well to hear what the Spirit is saying to the church.

Isaiah was given the assignment of being God's spokesman to a people who were religious to the bone.

The prophet Isaiah was a man with a holy vertical that stimulated an influential horizontal. His vertical *passion* for God created a horizontal *compassion* for those who are made in the

Christians in the Public Square

image of God. To say it another way, Isaiah's *connection* with deity fueled his *commitment* to humanity.

This passage of Scripture in Isaiah 58 lets us see God's perspective of ministry in the public square. It exposes the essence of true religion.

Today we need to answer the question, "Have we got good religion?" Good religion is Christ-centered ministry. The public square is desperately in need of good religion.

When the Gentiles came to Phillip and Andrew in John chapter 12, they made a statement that I believe speaks the heartcry of those in the public square desperate for spiritual reality. They said, "We would see Jesus."

Today perhaps more than ever before in the public square there are confused and hungering people who are saying "We would see Jesus."

They don't want to know if you line up with the moderates or the conservatives. They want to see if your life lines up with the life of Jesus.

They are not concerned with your position regarding women in the ministry. They want to see Jesus.

They are not asking if we are pro-life or pro-choice. They are asking to see Jesus. I am as pro-life as they come, but most hurting people aren't asking that question.

They don't want to see our denominational structures. They long to see Jesus.

These people are not impressed with how well you have memorized the "Roman Road." They would see Jesus.

They couldn't care less whether or not we have finished the "Experiencing God" course. They want to experience God through our lives.

They don't want to hear about how much Jesus loves them. They want to *see* the love of Jesus in the way we love them.

What I am trying say is that in today's public square talk is cheap and tradition is meaningless. *Helpless, hurting, and hopeless people are longing for an encounter with genuine love.*

I have been challenged to respond to a relevant question, "What Happens When Christians Do Make a Difference?" I believe the core of this question is this: "What are the effects of Christian obedience?"

Before turning specifically to our text in Isaiah 58, let me respond to this question quickly by saying that when Christians make a difference, the effects are seen in at least four ways: Jesus is magnified; believers are edified; sinners are justified; and Satan is terrified.

Have You Got Good Religion?

When believers and churches and conventions are right with God, operating in the power of the Holy Spirit, living lives of holiness and obedience, reconciled in their relationships, walking in redemptive love with their brothers and sisters, and aggressively intentional in sharing the good news of the gospel of Jesus Christ, there is an impact in heaven that brings forth a stirring in the church, that triggers a reverberation in the earth, thus causing a shake-up in the realms of darkness.

Paul Billheimer, in his book *Destined for the Throne,* shares some valuable insight regarding the potential of Christ's church to make a difference in society. Billheimer makes reference to the sending out of the seventy disciples in Luke 10. He writes:

> Following the return of the seventy and their jubilant report that even the demons were subject unto them, Jesus replies with a most amazing and startling statement, the significance of which apparently has escaped many believers. He first announced that he had personally witnessed Satan's expulsion from heaven. It was His word of authority that cast him forth so that Satan as lightning fell from heaven. Now He places in their hand that same word of authority. Now He is saying, "I hand this authority over to you." He said, "Behold, I give unto you power to tread on serpents and scorpions, and over all the power of the enemy; and nothing shall by any means hurt you."[1]

Billheimer goes on to say:

> This is the church's Magna Carta in her conflict with Satan. Here is a clear legal basis for deliverance from Satan's bondage and oppression, and for offensive action in the conflict with him. It is clear from this and other passages that God intends the true church, not Satan, to be the controlling factor in human affairs.[2]

I am convinced that the church will not impact the public square by means of the White House. We will only make a difference by way of the prayer house.

Our highest priority should not be to get a conservative judge on the U.S. Supreme Court. Our utmost desire must be to surrender our lives in humble service to the holy and solitary Judge of the sovereign court.

If we are going to have the kind of religion that will make an eternal difference, then we must have that good religion that Isaiah spoke of in our text. Isaiah was one of the great impact persons of the Old Testament. Isaiah was truly a "major prophet."

Christians in the Public Square

I think it is imperative to note that before Isaiah could impact his generation and every generation that has succeeded him in the past 2,700 years, he had to first be impacted by God. Isaiah shows us you cannot make a godly difference in others unless God has made a difference in you.

Isaiah was not prepared to make a difference in the public square of his day until he had a close encounter of the divine kind. (See Isaiah, chapter 6.)

Isaiah was God's mouthpiece, speaking to a proud, traditional, and religious people. Israel of Isaiah's day was similar to Laodicea of John's day. They perceived themselves to be rich and increased with goods and in need of nothing, but in reality they were wretched and miserable, poor, blind, and naked.

The theme of repentance resounds throughout Isaiah's prophecy, but in chapter 58 this theme seems to crystallize into a powerful challenge for the children of Israel to turn from their religiosity to a life of righteousness.

God says:

> Cry aloud, spare not, lift up thy voice like a trumpet, and shew my people their transgression, and the house of Jacob their sins. Yet they seek me daily, and delight to know my ways, as a nation that did righteousness, and forsook not the ordinance of their God: they ask of me the ordinances of justice; they take delight in approaching to God. Wherefore have we fasted, say they, and thou seest not? Wherefore have we afflicted our soul, and thou takest no knowledge? Behold, in the day of your fast ye find pleasure, and exact all your labours. Behold, ye fast for strife and debate, and to smite with the fist of wickedness: ye shall not fast as ye do this day, to make your voice to be heard on high. Is it such a fast that I have chosen? A day for a man to afflict his soul? Is it to bow down his head as a bulrush, and to spread sackcloth and ashes under him? Wilt thou call this a fast, and an acceptable day to the Lord? Is not this the fast that I have chosen? To loose the bands of wickedness, to undo the heavy burdens, and to let the oppressed go free, and that ye break every yoke? Is it not to deal thy bread to the hungry, and that thou bring the poor that are cast out to thy house? When thou seest the naked, that thou cover him; and that thou hide not thyself from thine own flesh? Then shall thy light break forth as the morning, and thine health shall spring forth speedily: and thy righteousness shall go before thee; the glory of the LORD

Have You Got Good Religion?

shall be thy reward. Then shalt thou call, and the LORD shall answer; thou shalt cry, and he shall say, Here I am. If thou take away from the midst of thee the yoke, the putting forth of the finger, and speaking vanity; and if thou draw out thy soul to the hungry, and satisfy the afflicted soul; then shall thy light rise in obscurity, and thy darkness be as the noonday: and the LORD shall guide thee continually, and satisfy thy soul in drought, and make fat thy bones: and thou shalt be like a watered garden, and like a spring of water, whose waters fail not. And they that shall be of thee shall build the old waste places: thou shalt raise up the foundations of many generation; and thou shalt be called, The repairer of the breach, The restorer of paths to dwell in (Isa. 58:1-12).

In this 58th chapter of Isaiah I believe God has provided for us a picture of what can happen when believers demonstrate good religion in the public square.

We can divide this portion of Scripture into three vital parts:

1. The Wrong Reasons for Religion (vv. 1-5)
2. The Right Reasons for Religion (vv. 6-7)
3. The Redemptive Results of Righteous Religion (vv. 8-12)

This passage opens with a divine command as God tells His prophet to, "Cry aloud, spare not, lift up thy voice like a trumpet, and shew my people their transgressions, and the house of Jacob their sins."

Quite obviously, the target audience of this message is not pagan people. The group in focus is God's chosen people.

In the succeeding verses God presents through Isaiah the wrong reasons for religion. *The Contemporary English Version* of the Scripture renders verses 2-4 this way:

> Day after day, you worship him and seem eager to learn his teachings. You act like a nation that wants to do right by obeying his laws. You ask him about justice, and say you enjoy worshiping the Lord. You wonder why the Lord pays no attention when you go without eating and act humble. But on those same days that you give up eating, you think only of yourselves and abuse your workers. You even get angry and ready to fight. No wonder God won't listen to your prayers!

First we can see that religion is wrong when we use it for the sake of intellectual enhancement rather than for spiritual advancement. There are those who study God as if He were a

Christians in the Public Square

college course. God spoke of these people when He said they draw near to Him with their lips but their hearts are far from Him.

But not only that, religion is also wrong when it disrespects the sovereignty of God. Notice in verse 3 the people had the audacity to say to God. "God, why have we fasted and you don't even see it, why have we suffered in our souls and you don't even notice our efforts?"

Some people try to use their religious activity as a means of manipulating God.

Still another characteristic to acknowledge from our text is that religion is wrong when it is used to exalt self and abase and abuse others. God says to these self-deceived religionists, "Look, you are fasting for personal convenience and to oppress those who work for you. You are making this carnal sacrifice so that you can promote strife and argument and to beat up on other people with your wicked religiosity."

As I hear these biting words of our text, I can't help but think of Christ's harsh rebuke of the scribes and the Pharisees. In Matthew 23:23-24 Jesus says:

> Woe unto you, scribes and Pharisees, hypocrites! For ye pay tithe of mint and anise and cummin, and have omitted the weightier matters of the law, judgment, mercy, and faith: these ought ye to have done, and not to leave the other undone. Ye blind guides, which strain at a gnat, and swallow a camel.

In our text God says the people were committing themselves to the intense physical discipline of fasting, going without food in a gesture of extreme sacrifice, but their efforts were vain because they had a zeal that was not according to knowledge.

These people that were the object of God's rebuke in our text could be categorized as wrongly religious zealots, and such persons have the capacity to give religion a bad name. They are disruptive and destructive people who dishonor the faith by invoking God's name to promote their own selfish agendas.

But religious zealotism does not always take the form of the sinister; it can also take the form of the sincere. Zeal has been defined as an "all-consuming passion."

When Jesus cleansed the temple in John chapter 2 the disciples remembered the scripture written in Psalm 69:9, "The zeal of thine house hath eaten me up."

Religious zeal is perhaps one of the most motivating and compelling forces known to man. While it obviously has the capacity to cause great harm in the public square, it also has the potential for producing great benefit.

Have You Got Good Religion?

There is a vital factor that determines whether a person's religion is good or bad, right or wrong—whether their zeal is sponsored by heaven or sponsored by hell. I choose to call that factor the glory factor. In other words, who gets the glory from the religious activity?

The prophet Jeremiah spoke to this issue quite eloquently in the 9th chapter and 23rd verse of his prophecy. It reads:

> Let not the wise man glory in his wisdom, neither let the mighty man glory in his might, let not the rich man glory in his riches: but let him that glorieth glory in this, that he understandeth and knoweth me, that I am the LORD which exercise lovingkindness, judgment, and righteousness, in the earth: for in these things I delight, saith the LORD.

As God continues to challenge His people in our text, we find that after presenting the wrong reasons for religion He goes on in verses 6 and 7 to present the right reasons for religion.

God says, "Is not this the fast that I have chosen? to loose the bands of wickedness, to undo the heavy burdens, and to let the oppressed go free, and that ye break every yoke? Is it not to deal thy bread to the hungry, and that thou bring the poor that are cast out to thy house?"

Perhaps one of the clearest definitions of religion can be found in James 1:27: "Pure religion and undefiled before God and the Father is this, To visit the fatherless and widows in their affliction, and to keep himself unspotted from the world."

In essence this passage is saying that good religion manifests itself in two primary ways: personal holiness and social compassion.

The fourth chapter of Luke records the account of Christ's prophetic visit to the synagogue in Nazareth. Luke 4:16-19 says:

> And he came to Nazareth, where he had been brought up; and, as his custom was, he went into the synagogue on the sabbath day, and stood up for to read. And there was delivered unto him the book of the prophet Esaias. And when he had opened the book, he found the place where it was written: The Spirit of the Lord is upon me, because he hath sent me to preach the gospel to the poor; he hath sent me to heal the brokenhearted, to preach deliverance to the captives, and recovering of sight to the blind, to set at liberty them that are bruised, to preach the acceptable year of the Lord.

Christians in the Public Square

Recently as I was pondering this passage I noticed something that I had somehow missed before. I noticed that the target population of Christ's ministry was the helpless and the hurting. Christ's ministry was attracted to poverty and pain.

One of the main problems in many of our ministries is that we are focusing upon the wrong population. We are targeting the middle class rather than the lowest class.

I believe it is safe to say that if you target the upper class you will have marginal impact on the upper class. If you target the middle class you will have impact upon the middle class and the upper class. But if you target the lowest class you will have impact upon every class.

If we, the people of God, are going to have a unique impact upon the urban public square, it is imperative that we do more than communicate Christ's love in conversation. We must actualize Christ's love by way of demonstration. If we are going to have a transforming effect upon the conditions of our society we must have a religion that is compassion-driven.

Someone said that:

Pity says, "I'm sorry you're hurt."
Sympathy says, "I'll hurt with you"
Compassion says, "I'll stick around till the hurt is gone."

If there was one characteristic that set Jesus' ministry apart from that of the religious elitists of His day it was that Jesus operated in compassion.

Matthew records in the ninth chapter of his Gospel that when Jesus saw the multitudes He was moved with compassion on them because they were harassed and helpless—like sheep wandering without a shepherd.

Jesus cared! Someone has said that people don't care how much you know until they know how much you care.

One of the great dangers in our pursuit of biblical integrity is the tendency to become more concerned with correctness than with compassion.

Colonel Doner has written a book entitled *The Samaritan Strategy* which deals with why the Christian Right Movement failed in the '70s and '80s. Doner writes:

Many Christian Right leaders, local pastors, and activists were motivated by a deep caring and concern for justice and righteousness, but it was not readily apparent to much of the Church and public at large. Christ sought to warn against this dilemma when He told us that people would recognize us as servants of God, empowered

Have You Got Good Religion?

and directed by Christ, by our love for one another and by our unity. Unfortunately, the Christian Right displayed precious little of either. The absence of a tangible, personalized love for our fellow man was disconcertingly noticeable. What proportion of our time and energy were we spending helping real people with real needs—the poor, the handicapped, the sick, the elderly, orphan, widow, the homeless, the abused, and the disadvantaged, the persecuted? To many, it did not appear that the Christian Right was legitimately concerned with these issues of compassion or even with the problems of real families struggling through the very trying problems of everyday life. Because our message was not perceived as being firmly rooted in a foundation of love and compassion, we lacked the moral authority to command loyalty and we lacked the vision to attract zeal, energy, and sacrifice."[3]

The New International Version translates Isaiah 58:6-7 this way:

Is not this the kind of fasting I have chosen: to loose the chains of injustice and untie the cords of the yoke, to set the oppressed free and break every yoke? Is it not to share your food with the hungry and to provide the poor wanderer with shelter—when you see the naked, to clothe him, and not to turn away from your own flesh and blood.

I believe there are at least four ways that good religion is defined in this potent passage of Scripture.

First, *good religion fights injustice.* Isaiah 58:6 says that those who are rightly religious give themselves to loosing the bonds of wickedness, undoing the heavy burdens, and letting the oppressed go free.

I believe that God has called His church to be a mighty band of freedom fighters. He has commissioned us to be the champions of justice for all people and especially for the poor and disenfranchised.

When God's people fail to respond to injustice they become contributors to social rebellion. The life of Absalom, the mutinous son of David, is a vivid example. When we consider the profile of Absalom we get the picture of an evil and deceptive degenerate whose selfish ambition prompted him to seek the overthrow and destruction of his own father. This assessment is definitely accurate. But while we cannot make an excuse for Absalom's

Christians in the Public Square

rebellion, we can surmise what made him so bad. Absalom's treachery was caused when a righteous man failed to respond to an injustice.

When David failed to respond to the rape of Tamar, the sister of Absalom, the young man decided to take matters into his own hands. In Absalom's story we can see that injustice led to anger, and anger led to bitterness, and bitterness led to vengeance, and vengeance led to rebellion, and rebellion led to destruction.

Injustice has produced some monsters in our society.

Today on the American scene there is a powerful Absalom who is struttin' his stuff in the face of the church. His name is Louis Farrakhan. We can brand him a heretic and a false prophet, and so he is, but the reality is that this egomaniac is partially the product of the evangelical church's failure to deal with social injustices.

But we learn from our text that not only does good religion fight injustice, it also *seeks to break bondages.*

If there is one form of bondage that is progressively sapping the very life of our society it is the bondage of drug addiction. I believe that God has called the church to set the drug captives free. But if we are going to truly make an impact in the war against drugs we have to expand the battle beyond the footsoldiers and crackheads in the urban ghetto. I contend that the drug problem in America is a poverty-tipped iceberg. To put it another way, I believe there is a diabolical chess game that is being played, and the black urban gangster is no more than a mere dispensable pawn. The kings and queens and bishops are far removed from the front lines.

If the drug war in America is going to be won it will be because wickedness in high places has been pulled down through the power of God's Holy Spirit. Corruption in government and in the corporate structure is perpetuating this devilish epidemic, and bold believers must target the real culprits.

Thirdly, good religion *responds to poverty.* God told His people that they were to distribute their food to the hungry and provide housing for the homeless. He said they were to demonstrate their religious zeal in providing clothing for those who were naked. In essence God was saying that genuine love for God manifests itself in meeting the basic needs of men. God wants us to live out a social gospel.

As we embark upon this subject of responding to poverty it is obvious that we are treading on some politically controversial ground. The issues of welfare reform and affirmative action are now front and center in the arena of political debate.

Have You Got Good Religion?

The majority of those who have identified themselves as the Christian Right have aligned themselves with conservative politicians who are calling for radical restructuring of welfare and the abolishing of affirmative action. There are those who are preaching this position with the same tenacity with which they preach the bodily resurrection of Jesus Christ from the dead.

This is a matter that has drawn much passion from the left as well as from the right. On the left side are those who are members of the Church of the Bleeding Heart, who see all poverty-stricken people as victims of the system, hopelessly in need of governmental care. But then there are those such as Mr. Limbaugh who have chosen to mock the poor and to paint them with a broad brush of criticism. They see all poor people as irresponsible leeches who live to beg and to blame others for their misfortune.

Charles Roesel, in his book *Meeting Needs, Sharing Christ*, made this observation:

> A smug and erroneous idea often expressed in religious circles is that if persons are poor, disadvantaged, oppressed, and needy, they are products of their own choices and therefore have received what they deserve. We often dismiss such persons as lazy, unwilling to help themselves, and unworthy of sympathy. We are especially vulnerable to this attitude when we are full, employed, and healthy.[4]

Roesel says further:

> We all know that some persons live on public assistance or go from one organization or church to another seeking a handout. Unfortunately, we permit these persons to influence our thinking so much that we generalize, concluding that all need and pain exist because these persons will not work and help themselves. This attitude is not only judgmental and unfair but also unbiblical and clearly unchristian. God has great compassion for the hurting and needy. Since He is a God of love and grace, He is concerned even for those whose sin and lack of character have caused their suffering. Therefore, even if persons' actions have led to their pain, we are not free to dismiss them as lazy, depraved, or unworthy. After all, who among us really deserves God's grace and love?[5]

It is obvious that Christ was a proponent of welfare, but at the same time He was an opponent of welfarism. Jesus fed the

Christians in the Public Square

5,000 in John chapter 6, but when they later came to make Him their "welfare king" He rejected the offer.

As to affirmative action, I believe that if the church would take the lead in fighting the sin of racism, then affirmative attitudes would become the basis for affirming actions.

In our text, Isaiah 58, God presents the wrong reasons for religion and the right reasons for religion. In verses 8-12 God shares with His beloved people the redemptive results of righteous religion.

Let's look at some of the highlights of the redemptive results of righteous religion:

• In verse 8 God says that He would give them a brand new day. He says, "Your light shall break forth as the morning."

• In verse 9 God says that He would give them prayer power. He says, "Then you shall call and the Lord will answer, You shall cry, and He will say 'Here I am.'"

• In verse 11 God promises that He would give them special guidance. He says, "And the Lord will guide you continually."

Finally in verse 12 God gives them the grand finale as He promises that if they practiced good religion then He would allow them to change the face of the public square. He would use them to restore righteousness to the land. God said, "And thou shalt be called, The repairer of the breach, The restorer of paths to dwell in." Like Nehemiah, they would rebuild the walls. Like Gideon, they would save the society.

I return to the original question: Have you got good religion?

Endnotes

[1] Paul Billheimer, *Destined for the Throne* (Minneapolis: Bethany House Publishers, 1975), 57.

[2] Ibid.

[3] Colonel V. Doner, *The Samaritan Strategy: A New Agenda for Christian Activists* (Brentwood, Tenn.: Wolgemuth and Hyatt, 1985), 41.

[4] Donald Atkinson and Charles Roesel, *Meeting Needs, Sharing Christ* (Nashville: Lifeway Press), 30.

[5] Ibid.

PASTORS FOR LIFE
Mobilizing for Scriptural Leadership

By Michael C. Cloer

The issue of abortion is not simply a political or social issue. The magnitude of the devastation caused by abortion is not only for the past twenty-three years, but also for those perpetual effects yet to be fully realized. It is my conviction that abortion is the most important issue facing the world today.

I am not trying to be sensational when I make that statement because I know there are some who will say, "What about the issue of race relations?" While that may be a very important social issue that the rights of certain minorities are being denied in America, I am telling you the rights of more than 1.5 million children are being taken away every year in America, never, ever to be returned. They are not just being denied their rights, they are being denied life.

Someone may say, "Well, what about the issue of hunger?" The World Health Organization estimates that 59 million abortions are done each year worldwide, whereas the highest estimate for the number who die yearly from hunger is 25 million. While hunger is a worldwide problem of great importance, there are twice the number of little children dying at the hands of merciless abortionists each year.

Some others might speak up and say, "What about world peace?" How does abortion rate with the threat of nuclear weapons, of war in this world? According to statistics, more than 28 million innocent babies have died in America's abortion chambers during the 23 years since the Supreme Court legalized abortion. By contrast, fewer than 1.4 million Americans have died in all of the armed conflicts and wars during our nation's entire

Christians in the Public Square

history. While I would not for one minute try to minimize the destruction of war, at the same time you must know that the bloodshed of war is a mere flesh wound compared to the legalized carnage of innocent, unborn babies. *Except for biopsies, abortion has become the most common surgical procedure performed in the United States of America.*

The question is, what can and should be done about this holocaust within biblical parameters? Without apology we can affirm that Jesus Christ is the only answer to abortion. To every person in any circumstance who considers abortion as an answer, we proclaim Jesus Christ, who is our hope and our salvation.

Therefore, since Jesus Christ is more powerful than the abortion industry, has more wealth than the abortion industry, and will still be Lord when the abortion industry is only gruesome history, I offer two simple premises for ending the slaughter of the innocents.

Premise One: The church is the only organization in America that can bring an end to the abortion holocaust.

After more than 20 years, abortion remains entrenched in American law and culture. There are still about 1.5 million surgical abortions per year, while estimates of chemical abortions caused by the pill, the IUD, Norplant, and Depo-Provera range from 5 to 20 million per year.

Clearly, the utilitarian and materialistic philosophies underlying abortion are deeply rooted in our society and are spreading, as evidenced by the rise of euthanasia, fetal experimentation, and genetic engineering. The fact is, the Judeo-Christian sanctity of life ethic is *quickly disintegrating* before our eyes. Is there any hope of reversing this downward spiral?

We believe there is.

The Lord Jesus Christ said, "I will build my church; and the gates of hell shall not prevail against it" (Matt. 16:18). We have long recognized that abortion mills are satanic strongholds, a literal representation of the very gates of hell on earth. That is the bad news.

The good news is that because Jesus Christ has said, "I *will*...," we can rejoice in the knowledge that *He is* personally going to do something about it. What He is doing is building His church, through which He will work to overcome the darkness.

The church—you and I—have a scriptural mandate that no other group has. The only hope of preserving our nation from its moral decay and the only hope of piercing the darkness is the church. Therefore, our emphasis in the pro-life movement must be upon the church, for Jesus Christ, who has all power in heaven and in earth, has promised it will prevail. Therein lies our hope and confidence.

Why should the church and a pastor be involved in pro-life ministry? What exactly is the relationship between the gospel of Jesus Christ and abortion? These are fair questions that deserve an answer, because pastors will sidestep abortion unless they are convinced there is a direct relationship between it and their gospel responsibilities.

In order to discuss the relationship between abortion and the gospel, we must first define some parameters. Abortion, the intentional killing of an unborn child anytime after fertilization, is the centerpiece of a myriad of problems. All that leads up to abortion (i.e., sexual immorality, anti-child mentality, etc.) and all that results from abortion (i.e. devaluation of human life, post-abortion syndrome, etc.) are related problems.

Pro-life ministry is the good news of Jesus Christ in response to abortion and these other abortion-related problems. Pro-life ministry addresses not only the act of child-killing, but the root causes and aftereffects as well. In essence, pro-life ministry takes the good news of Jesus Christ and seeks to contextualize it in response to abortion and abortion-related problems. Therefore, pastors should be involved in pro-life ministry because it is the gospel response to abortion, and the gospel is their calling.

Abortion is ugly, evil, and heartbreaking, but this does not hinder the saving work of God. In fact, the greater the darkness and distress appears, the brighter and stronger the light of the gospel becomes.

God is at work in pro-life ministry. If you are considering why you should get involved in pro-life ministry, or why you should increase your involvement, begin by understanding that pro-life ministry starts with God; it is part of His redemptive plan. God is at work in pro-life ministry, and as we see what the Father is doing, we have an opportunity to join Him in His work.

If you are doubtful that God is at work in pro-life ministry, consider the abundant evidence. First, unborn babies are saved from a violent, murderous death in pro-life ministry. If you think this to be insignificant, consider how you would feel about meeting such a death.

Second, mothers are saved in many different ways in pro-life ministry. They are saved from financial exploitation, physical injury, and emotional and psychological trauma. Most importantly, many are led to a saving knowledge of Jesus Christ. This takes place on the streets, in counseling centers, maternity

Christians in the Public Square

homes, adoption agencies, and many other aspects of pro-life ministry. Some crisis pregnancy centers (CPCs) lead more people to Jesus Christ than most churches do. This is not intended to be critical of the local church, but to underscore that pro-life ministry is an evangelistic outreach of the church that God is blessing.

These are the most visible results, but there are a multitude of other ways God is at work in pro-life ministry. Families are restored, babies are adopted, attitudes toward children are changed, and churches are renewed.

Proclaiming His righteousness. In addition, God is at work in pro-life ministry to raise His standard of righteousness, both in the church and in the world. God is holy, and the sixth commandment has not changed. God is making known to the world that His laws are both binding and nonnegotiable. The reason that we can never compromise on the morality and legality of child-killing is because God's Word will not allow it. Murder is forbidden.

God is also reminding the church that it must not shrink from its task to declare the truth, however unpopular it may be. Of course, this causes much controversy, not only in the world, but in the church as well. Nevertheless, the truth must be proclaimed boldly, without compromise, without apology.

Jesus told His disciples, "You are the salt of the earth.... You are the light of the world" (Matt. 5:13-14, NKJV). In the original language, Jesus intentionally used the emphatic pronoun to say, "You, and only you, are the salt of the earth.... Only you are the light of the world." It is time the church took our Lord's words seriously and quit waiting for the government, the schools, or any organization to do what only His church is scripturally mandated to do: Be salt and light!

Pro-life ministry is the church's response to abortion. It only makes sense that as leaders of the church, pastors must be involved. If a pastor has no concern for pro-life ministry, he is in essence saying that there is not gospel response to abortion. God forbid.

Premise Two: Pastors are the key to mobilizing the church.

It is the responsibility of pastors and elders to provide spiritual leadership for the local church. When pastors demonstrate leadership in some area of the gospel, their congregations usually follow their example. And when pastors fail to lead, their congregations usually follow that example as well.

Although others may step in to provide leadership when pastors fail, there can be no doubt that the local church is most effectively mobilized under pastoral leadership. Now is the time for pastors to lead.

Pastors For Life

Pastors For Life is based on the mandate of Micah 6:8 (NKJV).

He has shown you, O man, what is good;
And what does the LORD require of you
But to do justly, to love mercy,
And to walk humbly with your God?

Therefore, the mission of Pastors For Life is *to establish justice for the unborn and to show mercy to people in pregnancy-related situations by mobilizing the church through an organization of pastors, missionaries, and lay leaders.*

The church must respond to abortion both by working to establish justice and by showing mercy. Efforts to establish justice include legislation, education, and public witness through activities such as prayer, sidewalk counseling, and picketing. The church must also show mercy through crisis pregnancy centers, maternity homes, and adoption agencies.

All these and other aspects of pro-life ministry need to be done as we walk humbly before God. This means, of course, that we must begin in the church before we point at anyone else. We must pray and preach and live the truth about abortion in the church before we can address the world with integrity. Walking humbly means we repent of our own failures. It also means we will depend entirely upon *God* for the victory. We will submit to civil authority whenever possible, and we will reject the use of violence or vandalism. May God help us to repent of our own sins.

A pastor may be convinced that pro-life ministry is a good idea in general, but remain unconvinced about the need for his involvement in a group such as Pastors For Life. So the question arises, why should a pastor be involved specifically in Pastors For Life? After all, are there not many other aspects of pro-life ministry just as important?

Certainly, pro-life ministry is multifaceted and there are many avenues of involvement. If a pastor is already deeply committed to another aspect of pro-life ministry, let him continue serving there as long as God wills.

There is a unique aspect to Pastors For Life, however, that every pastor should consider when deciding whether to be involved.

That is, *Pastors For Life is not a para-church organization; rather it is the local church in action.* It provides local pastors a vehicle to come together and call on the Lord as elders in the gates of the city. The direction of Pastors For Life is determined by local pastors, and they control the decision-making process. For pastors with a burden for pro-life ministry, Pastors For Life provides an

Christians in the Public Square

avenue of involvement which is church-oriented and pastor-led. It provides an ideal mechanism for pastors to "plug in" to what God is doing in their area in pro-life ministry.

This does not mean that pastors won't also be involved in other pro-life groups. Many pastors work with crisis pregnancy centers, maternity homes, and other pro-life ministries. Their involvement in other ministries enriches the perspective of Pastors For Life, as well as providing these ministries with a good contact point to local pastors. Pastors can serve in these other ways and still be a part of Pastors For Life, meeting with other pastors and leading their own congregation in a cooperative, area-wide effort. This enables Pastors For Life to provide area-wide leadership for pro-life ministry that benefits everyone.

A pastor should be involved in Pastors For Life because it is the most effective means of mobilizing the church for pro-life ministry. Pastors For Life will equip a pastor to lead his own congregation in pro-life ministry, and enable him to work with other pastors and churches as well.

Here's how Pastors For Life works:

Step One: Pastors of all denominations meet together on a regular basis to pray and prepare to lead their congregations in pro-life ministry. A leadership team, comprised of pastors who are willing to take on extra responsibility, provides direction for the group.

Once plans have been made, each pastor determines to what extent he will lead his church in any particular activity. This allows pastors to be a part of the group, while maintaining freedom in leading their respective churches.

Step Two: Pastors may call a full-time pro-life missionary to work under their leadership, assisting them in all aspects of pro-life ministry. Missionaries propose strategic plans to the leadership team, as well as overseeing the day-to-day operations.

Since pastors are under heavy time demands, missionaries are critically needed to keep the ministry organized and moving forward. Missionaries are fully accountable to pastors, who should assume the final responsibility for funding them.

Step Three: In addition to pastors and missionaries, lay leaders also have an important role to fulfill. By coming alongside their own pastor and offering help, lay leaders can handle many of the details of pro-life ministry within their church.

In order to keep lay leaders updated, Pastors For Life holds a separate meeting for them whenever the pastors meet. This way,

Pastors For Life

pastors and lay leaders receive the same information and can coordinate their efforts.

If a pastor chooses not to be involved in Pastors For Life, a lay leader can step forward to provide leadership in that church, as long as it meets the pastor's approval.

Pastors For Life is not a short-term approach to responding to abortion. Abortion is well rooted in our culture, and the self-centered, anti-child mentality behind abortion has deeply infected the church also. We cannot expect to "fix" the problem overnight. Reversing the progress of groups such as Planned Parenthood requires a long-term commitment to changing hearts and minds at the local level, beginning in the church and working outward.

Pastors For Life provides a way for like-minded pastors to make that commitment together by meeting on a regular basis for prayer and planning on how they can establish justice and show mercy for the preborn.

The critical need of the hour is for men who refuse to accept the status quo, men who refuse to live in peace with the child-killers in their community. Until pastors have a spiritual-warfare mentality that says, "NIMBY (Not In My Back Yard)," our communities will continue to be decimated by child-killing.

> The Church is responsible for the religious life of the city, for the moral standards of the city, for the social order of the city. If you can persuade me that we have no responsibilities, that the Church exists merely for the conserving of the life of her own members, then I will leave the Church, and join with others who have a keener sense of moral and religious responsibility; in the light of the New Testament teaching.... The Church is against the city as it is, in order to make the city what it ought to be. The Church lifts her voice in protest against iniquity in the city or nation, because her business is to make the city and the nation what God would have them to be.
> (G. Campbell Morgan, 1912)

ENGAGING THE LOCAL PUBLIC SQUARE

By Daniel R. Heimbach

Let me tell you the story of a Christian who became engaged in the public square. This is a true story, a real story. It begins with a married man, a responsible father of young children, busy with family life. He is also a Christian, active in his local church, whose life revolves around Christian ministry.

This Christian father busy in Christian service becomes increasingly conscious of a negative drift in the surrounding culture. Soon this awareness rises to alarm as specific developments affecting his own family and ministry take a distinctly anti-Christian turn. As he thinks and prays about these developments, he feels a growing desire, a desire which then takes the shape of a call to do something about it. He decides to seek public office. He declares his candidacy. He runs a spirited campaign. And, he wins the election.

If you ask, he would tell you that what motivates his engagement with the public square is only superficially civil and economic. At a deeper and more profound level, the incentives that energize him are moral and religious. Generally speaking, he is involved in the public square for three reasons. First, he is involved to make a positive impact on society in line with the sort of moral leadership upon which this nation was founded. Second, he is involved to resist the forces of immorality that are corroding the traditional moral consensus upon which the strength and

Christians in the Public Square

health of society depend. Third, he is involved to keep anti-Christian/anti-historical/anti-moral elements in our democracy from using the power of government to encroach upon the freedom and welfare of Christian families and Christian institutions.

Does this story sound familiar? It should, because it might easily be the story of any number of men and women now engaged in national-level politics. Presidential candidates such as Pat Buchanan, Richard Lugar, and Alan Keyes come to mind. It could also be the story of some of our distinguished congressional leaders—senators such as Dan Coats of Indiana, Trent Lott of Mississippi, and Jesse Helms of North Carolina, or congressmen such as Henry Hyde of Illinois, Chris Smith of New Jersey, and David McIntosh and Mark Souder of Indiana.

But the story I have told is *not* the story of someone in national office. Rather, it is a story from grass-roots, local politics. It is a story about Christian involvement in the public square at the level of small-town, municipal government, at the level where the public square is nearest the life of our families, nearest the life of our local churches, and nearest the life of Christian private schools and seminaries. I have been telling you my own story of last year when I decided to run for office and was elected a commissioner for the town of Wake Forest in the state of North Carolina, a town whose population is only just over 7,000.

I am a Christian father, an ordained minister of the gospel, and a full-time member of the faculty at Southeastern Baptist Theological Seminary, where I teach Christian ethics. But I am also an American citizen, a neighbor active in local community affairs, and now also an elected government official serving at the local level. While the kleig lights of media attention are appropriately focused on national politics, and while God certainly calls men and women of faith to be salt and light in the arenas of national government, let me highlight as well the importance of responsible Christian involvement at the local level.

Think with me for a minute. At what level is government most directly involved in the education of our children and in deciding the moral standards they are taught or made to live by? At what level is government most directly tied to family life? At what level is government most directly involved in policing individual behavior? At what level does government have the greatest impact on whether, where, or how we build facilities needed to accommodate our churches, missionary programs, schools, and seminaries? The answer to each of these questions is local municipal or county government.

The strategic importance of local government cannot be

Engaging the Local Public Square

denied. No large-scale change in national policy is secure without winning the local level. No national policy direction can be sustained without acceptance and support at the local level. And no national policy can ever reach all the many matters affecting daily life covered at the local level. This means Christians must not dismiss the importance of local politics. Not only does local politics offer a greater number of opportunities for Christian involvement in the public square; in most cases it affords opportunities to gain a more immediate, and in some cases an even more telling impact on the life and welfare of individuals, families, and neighborhoods.

To demonstrate the sort of opportunities that can be found at the local level, let me give three examples from my own recent experience. I was motivated to run for town commissioner when the seminary at which I teach was denied a request to rezone its landholdings for sale and development. The seminary is the largest institution in our small town, and it has for years owned a tract of undeveloped land which came with the purchase, some forty years ago, of what was the original campus of Wake Forest University.

Despite talk about the separation of church and state in American law, the local situation in Wake Forest was affected by religious feelings that appeared to have some influence on decisions of town government. Moreover, this influence had become opposed to the life and ministry of the seminary. While the institutions of church and state were not linked in any direct way, religious resentment arising from theological realignment at the seminary was one of several factors behind the town's denial.

Although the theological course taken by religious institutions is not a civil matter, and the seminary's change in theological direction had nothing to do with the secular business of town government, religious polarization was part of the reason the town was moved to hazard its own economic stability in opposition to seminary development. I decided to run for office because I am a town resident interested in restoring responsible secular leadership to municipal government. But, I was also motivated as a Christian who wanted to temper the attitude of spiritual hostility evident in the public square.

A second example from my own experience has to do with becoming involved with the local school board. Not long after arriving in North Carolina, I was introduced to the person who chairs the Wake County Board of Education. This particular school board is rather strategic in the state of North Carolina, since it covers the capital city of Raleigh and the entire region

Christians in the Public Square

surrounding the capital area. The chairman also happens to be a member of my church. Because I had some experience with policy task forces and have a background in ethics, but also because she trusted my judgment as a Christian, she asked me to help set up a task force to reintroduce character education into our public schools. I accepted her offer, and so began my work with the Wake County Board of Education Character Education Task Force.

This work involved bringing together a cross section from the local community—parents, community activists and public school administrators, all coming from different religious perspectives, different cultural traditions, and different political philosophies. But out of their diversity, the members of this task force were asked to find common ground on which to renew general community support for public school instruction that could again: (1) affirm a fixed difference between right and wrong, (2) advocate right over wrong, and (3) recognize the importance of praising and modeling good character. Of course, this effort took direct aim at the "values clarification" thinking that over the last several decades has turned American public schools into wastelands of moral relativity—wastelands in which moral standards apply only if you like them, in which no moral standards can really be true or false, in which no values, however noble or perverse, can be judged better or worse, and in which moral accountability is replaced by an emphasis on self-fulfillment and the authenticity of personal desires.

Does a task force for character education sound hopeless? Let me tell you what we achieved. Although moral judgments are always framed by religious convictions—convictions about human nature and ultimate reality—and although it must not be the business of teachers in public schools to advocate religious convictions contrary to what parents teach their children at home, we found there is a large area of public agreement concerning desirable traits of personal character. Despite many different philosophical and religious points of view, we found common ground, in the public square, for advocating a wide range of traits we have traditionally called "virtues."

Because we wanted to guard against efforts to promote deviancy in the name of "character education," and because we wished to affirm the priority of parents over public schools in matters of moral instruction, we chose to restrict character education in public schools to the promotion of virtues that had broad community support. By insisting on unanimous consent by all members of the task force, and by backing it with a questionnaire to all parents with children in our public schools, we

Engaging the Local Public Square

ended up with broad public backing for a program focused on eight character traits: courage, good judgment, integrity, kindness, perseverance, respect, responsibility, and self-discipline. These traits are now advocated in all Wake County public schools, and the task force continues to monitor their implementation.

The third example from my experience as a Christian engaging the public square at the local level has to do with taking part in grass-roots political party organizations. Whether you are Democrat or Republican, you will find the political parties cannot function without the dedicated help of many volunteers. Indeed these grass-roots workers are the heart of our political system. No political party in America can succeed without them. These volunteers do not attract much attention, but they can be very influential in the process of selecting candidates for office, in setting policy priorities within their party, in registering new voters, and in educating voters in their local districts.

Since moving to North Carolina, I have become a part of the Republican party organization for that state. I do this as a matter of civic duty because it is my privilege as an American citizen. But I am also motivated to be involved because it is an opportunity for me, as a Christian, to be salt and light in the political leadership of my community. Of course, my ultimate allegiance is to Jesus Christ, and Jesus does not answer to any political party. But citizen involvement in American politics means you have to pick a horse to ride in order to join the race. The horse I ride is the Republican horse, but I know brothers and sisters in Christ who are Democrats, and I am pleased they are trying to be faithful in a different political structure. My point is that involvement in political party organizations can be a way Christian citizens make a positive contribution in the public square.

Just recently, the difference this involvement makes was proven dramatically when the Republican Party of North Carolina elected a new state chairman. The winning candidate, the new leader of the Republican Party in North Carolina, was elected by a one-vote margin. Since he was the candidate I supported, my one vote made a very *big* difference. If I had not been there, he would not have been elected chairman, and the Republican Party in North Carolina would now be heading in a slightly different direction.

Christians *can* make a difference by their involvement in the public square. Even if others do not recognize the difference you are trying to make, and even if the opportunity to have real impact seems hopeless, I still urge the importance of putting faith into practice in the arenas of public life. Why? One reason is that we

Christians in the Public Square

have in the United States a form of government that is *of* the people, *by* the people, and *for* the people. This means your involvement is expected in order to maintain the common good. But, there is an even more important reason Christians must be involved in public life, and that is because it is also a matter of being faithful—being faithful to the God who calls us to be salt and light, to the God who expects us to seek the welfare of those cities in which He places us, to the God who says He expects us to live as "sons of God, without rebuke, in the midst of a crooked and perverse nation, among whom ye shine as lights" (Phil. 2:15).

As you consider how you might be involved in the public square, I recommend starting where you are. For many, your best opportunity may come at the level of local government. Pray about it. Do not pack your bags for Washington too quickly. You may discover you have opportunities to make a strategic impact right where you are. I pray that you will.

TRANSFORMING THE BLACK CHURCH IN SUBURBIA

By E.W. McCall, Sr.

"Church" is a word that brings to the minds of different persons and people groups a myriad of meanings. Sadly, too many have not seen what this word meant during the first century, or what it will mean during the twenty-first century. This problem is heightened when we observe what is meant by the word "church" in the Black church, especially when it is located in suburbia. The church is often seen only as a place to sing, pray, and preach. Though these occur, they should not be viewed as the total meaning of the church. The church is really not a place, but a group of baptized believers assembled to render praises to God and service to humanity.[1]

What makes the Black church so different in suburbia is that there is, for the most part, no defined community. The suburban Black church is populated by a mixture of the people in that community or region, not a church comprised only of people who are Black. The worshipers come from miles around. They live in the bedroom communities, cities often up to fifty miles away, in all directions from the church. These congregants come from the inner city, and some come from small towns and even different denominations. This too contributes to the confusion over the meaning and idea of church.

However the problem, the suburban Black church cannot be excused from fulfilling the biblical idea of what the church is and

Christians in the Public Square

must be during the twenty-first century: a community of believers which has been gathered from the inhabitants of a specific area.

The community meets in assembly, to be sure, but it is constituted as *ecclesia* prior to and apart from such assemblies. The "church" idea found in the minds and hearts of the believers in the Black church located in suburbia must be radically changed to meet the needs as well as the demands which will be placed upon her during the twenty-first century.

Why Do the Demands of the Times Dictate a Transformation of the Suburban Black Church?

As we think about the times and the demand for transformation, we must consider that there are different kinds of demands found in the time in which we live. There is first of all a biblical demand placed upon us by our Lord in Matthew 25:31-34. This text seems to stress this fact. A careful reading of our text will soon reveal that the Lord was no doubt on the Mount of Olives, thinking as He was looking upon the Holy City and even the temple. While sitting there, He seems to think about the Jewish leadership's rejection of His being sent by the Father as the Messiah. Calvary, in three days, would be His to endure. At almost this final hour, He speaks of Himself as King. He tells us what it will be like on that day of judgment, when we shall give an account of our time as Christians here on earth. Listen as He says, "Then shall the King say unto them on His right hand, Come ye blessed of my Father, inherit the kingdom prepared for you from the foundation of the world" (v. 34). And so, our biblical demand is that we at the end be acceptable to Him. We sure don't want Him to say to us as He did in verse 41, "Depart from me," because we failed to see what it meant to be the church.

Another demand that is clearly part of our time is the needs our people will have because of the pervasive cutbacks in programs and services. No longer can the Black community in particular, and the whole of America in general, depend on government to take care of all our needs and wants. The Black church must see the need to transform itself into a force to deal with holistic approaches to ministry. We must understand we are not only to be a place where the power is found to change people to become followers of Christ, but the Black church in suburbia in this generation and on into the twenty-first century must see herself as a station of empowerment.

Because we in suburbia are located miles away from many of the vital services, with the cutbacks and downsizing of government goods and services will come an even greater need to transform the

Transforming the Black Church in Suburbia

church to fill those vacancies left by the government and big business. One may ask, what are some of the ways the Black church in suburbia must transform herself? Here I must begin to speak from my personal convictions and experiences. The church that we speak of here must offer some, if not all, of the following opportunities so members of the church as well as the community can be empowered and empower themselves:

1. *A 12-Step Drug Program.* We can no longer pretend that drugs have not made it to the suburbs. There is not enough money for the government to handle all of the problematic concerns wrought on our society by the drug culture. We cannot sit idly by and watch our sons, daughters, mothers, and fathers self-destruct. The Black church must develop halfway houses so those who have been imprisoned can be released to have a fair chance to transition back into society.

2. *Tutorial Programs.* Too often we have said to the schools, "Take our children, educate them, teach them about sex, right, wrong, and be sure to help them to become responsible citizens." Well, we all have seen the damaging results of that mind-set: children who cannot read, write, calculate, or spell, babies having babies and, even worse, young girls *killing* their babies before they are born. We must tell them that safe sex is found only in the marriage relationship.

3. *Midnight Basketball.* Many of our youth don't have anything to do. To burn up the energy that would be used in a destructive manner, midnight basketball is a healthy alternative. For those who would follow a more structured program, an inter-church league program would be most beneficial.

4. *Homeless Food Program.* Sometimes we look in suburbia, and we somehow see no people who are without food, clothing, or shelter. Yet there are people without these vital necessities of life. It is important to set up local programs and travel back into the city on Skid Row where these needs are clearly present. These programs should operate on a weekly basis.

5. *Preschool Day-care, Elementary After-school Programs.* All such programs are needed to give our children and youth a fair chance in life.

The above are just some of the social programs that we have at St. Stephen Missionary Baptist Church in La Puente, California. One thing has become so clear to me. There are social concerns which can be expressed better at the local level, by the church, if the church is willing to transform herself. However, we must admit that government still has a role to play, especially when there is no visible church to carry on such programs. The

Christians in the Public Square

church's primary reason for being is not social, but its main function is to save men, women, boys, and girls from the grips of Satan and to strengthen them to be more like Christ. Thus, we must continue to work on the demands to be the church that Christ is looking for in these latter days.

What Principles Should Guide the Transformation of the Black Church in Suburbia?

Jesus, in these verses, highlights some specific areas of mercy which He counts as being indicators of those who have truly been part of the transforming process as one of His. Listen as He says in Matthew 25:35-36, "For I was an hungered, and ye gave me meat: I was thirsty, and ye gave me drink: I was a stranger, and ye took me in: naked, and ye clothed me: I was sick, and ye visited me: I was in prison, and ye came unto me." If we understand what Jesus is saying to those then (and in a sense to those of us now), He is bringing to our minds the forms of ministry in which He performed while with them for the last three years. They are not by any means an exhaustive list of ministries to be done by them; they are the kinds of ministries which express the heart and mind of His disciples then and now. We see them as indicators of one's willingness to show pity, even sympathy, charity, or denial of self. What our Lord says, in a sense is, "You show Me your works and it is in this you show Me your faith."

The transformation that is needed to accomplish this supreme grace of love mentioned in Matthew 25:35-36 cannot be fulfilled unless the church is willing to follow some practical principles which will lead to change. John P. Kotter gives us some principles[2] which I think will help to produce this transformation with a degree of conscientiousness. Although these are principles which are used in the business world, I believe we can find theological meaning behind each of them.

1. *Establishing a Sense of Urgency*. This sense of urgency must first be found in our willingness to share Jesus *now*. People are dying by the thousands every minute, going to hell because there are still those people who don't see the urgency of telling souls about the saving grace of Jesus. Kotter says,

> Most successful change efforts begin when some individual or groups start to look hard at a company's competitive situation, market position, technological trends, and financial drop when an important patent expires, the five-year trend in declining margins in core business, or an emerging market that everyone seems to ignore. They then find ways to communicate this

Transforming the Black Church in Suburbia

information broadly and dramatically, especially with respect to crises, potential crises, or great opportunities that are very timely. This first step is essential because just getting a transformation program started requires the aggressive cooperation of many individuals. Without motivation, people won't help and the effort goes nowhere.[3]

If the Black church in suburbia is going to transform, there must be a sense of urgency on the part of the leadership and people. It does not matter whether this is to carry out witnessing to a lost world about Jesus, or ministering to the needs of those who are without food, shelter, clothing, in prison, or find themselves needing to understand how to live life.

2. *Forming a Powerful Guiding Coalition.* Kotter further states, "In cases of successful transformation efforts, the leadership coalition grows and grows over time. Also, a high sense of urgency within the managerial ranks helps enormously in putting together a guiding coalition."[4] Now this is especially true in the Black church. Unless the pastor is part and party to the transformation, very little is going to happen in the coalition.

3. *Creating a Vision.* The guiding coalition now is called upon to create a vision to communicate to the church at large. A vision says something that helps clarify the direction in which an organization needs to move. When the vision has been clarified, the people, for the most part, will get behind the vision. Money and strategies can be worked out to fulfill the vision. The church must catch hold of the vision to reach, witness, and minister to the needs of people.

4. *Communicating the Vision.* Using every vehicle possible to communicate the new vision and strategies should be a high priority. The church must be seen by the guiding coalition, which in this case has to include the pastor, as a business. We are in the business of saving souls for the kingdom. In every aspect of church life this vision must be communicated.

Some of the areas of the church that should communicate this new vision should include: The Mission, Deacon's Ministry, Sunday School Department, Music Department, and of course, the pastor and administrative staff.

5. *Empowering Others to Act.* In order that others may be empowered to act, Kotter says that several things must happen:

(a) Get rid of obstacles to change.

(b) Change systems or structures that seriously undermine the vision.

Christians in the Public Square

(c) Encourage risk-taking and nontraditional ideas, activities, and actions.[5]

Now to accomplish this end often calls for the reassignment, or even the resigning, of certain people in order for the vision to go forward. Sometimes this person may be a person who has held a position for a very long time, and they view change as a way of pushing them out. It is here much prayer should be rendered as to how one should do the loving, kind, and Christian thing.

6. *Planning for and Creating Short-Term Vision.* Real transformation takes time, and a renewal effort risks losing momentum if there are no short-term goals to meet and celebrate. Most people will not go on the long march unless they see compelling evidence, within twelve to twenty-four months, that the journey is producing expected results. Well, this time frame may work well in the wider world, but in the Black church in suburbia results must be found where all can see it in twelve months or less. It does not matter if it is a new ministry or a building program to house new ministries, immediate results must be seen if you want the financial and even physical support to continue. We seem to be saturated with what I call "microwave mentality." We want what we want and we want it now. Kotter makes it clear: "Create Short-Term Wins."[6] The latter is passive, the former is active. In a successful transformation managers actively look for ways to obtain clear performance, improvements, establish goals in the yearly planning system, achieve the objectives, and reward the people involved with recognition, promotion, and even money. This principle and way of recognizing people for their achievement can and should be used by the church to make those involved get the sense of real progress.

7. *Consolidating Improvements and Producing Still More Change.* Here Kotter states that, after planning for short-term wins, we must be willing to use increased credibility to change systems, structures, and policies that do not fit the vision. Often this requires hiring, promoting, and developing employees who can implement the vision, as well as reinvigorating the process with new projects, themes, and change agents.[7]

The Black church in suburbia, and the church in general, would do well to consider what Kotter is suggesting here in this seventh step. Too often we meet success on some short victory and we declare victory too soon. At St. Stephen, we find hiring new employees is not always the answer, since the majority of our work in ministry is done by unpaid staff people. We must be willing to reassign and even ask some unpaid staff persons who are in the way of vision to step aside so those who understand the

Transforming the Black Church in Suburbia

transformation goals the church has in mind can proceed.

What Kotter means by using credibility is that the leadership should use the short-term wins to tackle even bigger problems. These short-term victories, when used properly, will enable you to go after systems and structures that are not consistent with the transformation vision of the church. One of the major problems we find in the Black church is the carryover of the way things were done in the past. Because traditionally in the Black church people seem to remain in one position all their lives, change comes very slowly. The deacon chairman often remains for life. Thus transforming the Black church, in some cases, may become impossible. One victory that must be reached is to change the way leadership is rotated to meet the vision and transforming efforts of the church. If the system of rotating and changing the chairman of deacons can be changed, this change can be used to propel the church to tackle other changes needed in reassigning persons who will not be productive in implementing the vision.

8. *Instituting New Approaches.* When these steps are followed, you can communicate to the paid and the unpaid staff how things need to be done. They will be able to see the connection between changed behavior and the success the church has experienced. If this can be seen and understood by those in place now, you have successfully institutionalized change.

These new approaches, though they are found in the business world to a large extent, are most useful in the local church. The Black church found in suburbia will more likely be able to institute the new approaches because of the kind and quality of people the Black church has to draw from to be part of the church membership.

As often as you can, show the connection between what is happening and what was happening before the transformation took place. This will be most helpful in institutionalizing the change. Changes that can be expected from this transformation are: increased membership, more committed workers, higher budget, excitement among the membership, an overall excitement of what is happening in the church now.

The eight steps mentioned are not a cure-all for all the problems of the church, but they can do much in transforming the church to be the church for the twenty-first century.

Who Is Responsible for This Transformation of the Black Church in Suburbia?

In light of the present mind-set of society and even many Black Southern Baptists, this question must be answered. The

Christians in the Public Square

same mind-set that people have in society, they often bring into the church. There are those in society who feel that Washington will, can, and should solve all of their needs. They think Washington can raise their children, feed their families, and correct what is wrong in their communities. This is the mind-set we find in many of those who are a part of our membership in the Black church in suburbia.

Since this seems to be a profound problem in the Black church, who is responsible for this transformation? In light of the past history of racism in America and the Southern Baptist Convention, who is responsible for this transformation needed in the Black church in suburbia? Well, the persons responsible for this transformation are not the Southern Baptist Convention, nor its agencies. The responsible persons can be none other than the Black church itself—the pastor, deacons, teachers, WMU, Brotherhood, Music Department, in short, the church.

It is my firm belief that what is wrong and even paralyzing is to think that some outside source is going to transform that which can only be transformed by those who are a part of the church. Transformation is an internal thing, done by the will and ability of the people and the leadership. We must, if transformation is to be seen in the Black church, face our problems and then seek ways to fix them. We cannot fix them until we face them with our abilities, resources, and the Power from on high. If we remain "underlings" in the church world, the fault is not in others but in ourselves. We have in suburbia some of the best minds in the land; we even have resources and budgets to support this transformation. Now what is left to do is to utilize our will to change, allocate the proper resources, and get involved in the areas of the Convention that will help bring about the change that will transform our churches to be able to meet the needs of our members and community.

Who Will Benefit from This Transformation of the Black Church in Suburbia?

It goes without saying that the kingdom of God would benefit from such a radical departure from the past. However, in more specific terms, who will benefit from this transformation of the Black church in suburbia? First, I feel the members of that congregation will benefit. They will see a greater commitment of themselves to the church and the kingdom of God. They will be more willing to get involved in ministry with meaning. These same people would experience what it means to hear the words of our Lord in Matthew 25:37-40, when the righteous asked,

Transforming the Black Church in Suburbia

When saw we thee an hungered, and fed thee? or thirsty, and gave thee drink? When saw we thee a stranger, and took thee in? or naked, and clothed thee? Or when saw we thee sick, or in prison, and came unto thee? And the King shall answer and say unto them, Verily I say unto you, Inasmuch as ye have done it unto one of the least of these my brethren, ye have done it unto me.

So who will benefit from this transformed church in suburbia? Any and all persons who can be seen as those whom Jesus called the least of these.

There is another benefit that can be highlighted from this transformation. The community where the church is located will truly benefit. Crime will go down because of the outreach ministries among our youth and even the adult population. Social services at the church, which were long ago left in the inner city, will enhance the quality of life of the community. Because the Black church in suburbia is part of the Southern Baptist Convention, when the Black church in suburbia is transformed, the Convention will benefit. The Convention will have had a greater role in kingdom building. Baptisms will increase, monies given in our cooperative effort will be higher, because of the larger budgets of this transformed church. Finally, who will benefit? Only the Lord knows all who will benefit from the Black church transformed in suburbia.

How Can the Southern Baptist Convention Help Usher in This Transformation Needed in the Black Church in Suburbia?

Although it is the responsibility of the suburban Black church, its leaders, and members at large to transform the church, the Southern Baptist Convention has a definite role to play. The Southern Baptist Convention must see itself in the role of a change-agent—an agent with resources, training opportunities, materials, and personnel available—for these churches in suburbia, as it does for all churches. The Southern Baptist Convention must make all that she has to offer open to all those churches who are a part of the Convention. Budget allocations must be seen as fair. Involvement in the Convention must be looked at anew to see how more representation of suburban Black churches can be achieved in the best and largest convention in America.

Transforming the Black church is so vital to those Blacks, and even others, who have moved to suburbia. In a real sense the Black church is not a church comprised of only people who are

Christians in the Public Square

Black. The suburban Black church is populated by a mixture of the people in that community or region. This representation is most notable when the church seeks to transform itself, as Jesus described what a transformed church should become in Matthew 25:31-40.

Endnotes

[1] George Authur Buttrick, *The Interpreter's Dictionary of the Bible* (Nashville: Abingdon, 1962), 608.

[2] John P. Kotter, "Leading Change: Why Transformation Efforts Fail," *Harvard Business Review*, March-April, 1995.

[3] Ibid., 60.

[4] Ibid., 63.

[5] Ibid.

[6] Ibid.

[7] Ibid.

HOPE FOR THE HURTING

By Charles Roesel

These were days of great excitement in Capernaum. A new teacher with awesome power was in town. The mere mention that he was near was enough to gather a crowd. When the word spread that he was in a certain house, the people came from everywhere, jamming the house to capacity.

Suddenly, as Jesus was preaching, there was the thud of falling mud and the sound of drifting thatch. Every eye turned to the ceiling. There they saw a hole and four men making it larger. These men took sashes from their waists and tied the sashes to four corners of the stretcher on which a paralytic lay.

Imagine the four men falling on their faces, gazing down through the hole to see what Jesus would do. They had done all they could; they had brought the man to Jesus. Now they were trusting in Jesus to do that which only He could do.

When Jesus saw their faith, He turned to the paralyzed man and said, "Son, your sins are forgiven."

Immediately a chill in the air could be sensed. The religious leaders were saying: "Who does this man think He is? He's offering to forgive sins—only God can do that! Besides, this man has not come for forgiveness, but for healing."

Jesus, perceiving their thoughts, said: "Which is it easier for me to do? To say, 'Your sins be forgiven,' or to say, 'Arise, take up your bed, and walk'? But, so that you may know that the Son of Man has authority to forgive sins,..." then He said to the paralyzed man, "Arise, take up your bed, and walk" (Mark 2:1-11).

Christians in the Public Square

The man arose, took up his bed, and walked. It was a glorious hour, one that has many lessons in it for us.

1. First of all, we see the *hurting*—the man that was paralyzed. We never knew the magnitude of the problem of hurting people until we became involved in ministry-based evangelism. Little did we realize that in a town of 30,000 people, when we started our Rescue Mission, we would minister to more than 5,000 people per year who need shelter, food, clothing, work, and, most of all, a saving encounter with Jesus Christ. Sometimes our parking lot looks like a scene from *The Grapes Of Wrath:* families with children filling old, dilapidated station wagons, their eyes glazed with a strange stare of despair.

Little did we realize when we began our Pregnancy Care Center that, in a small community like ours, we would average more than 100 per month coming for testing, counseling, maternity clothes, and baby supplies. We never knew, when we established our Women's Shelter, that the first week the shelter was open, it would be filled to capacity.

Once Billy Graham, in preparation for a crusade, wrote to ask the community leaders for a list of the hurting people for whom he and his team could pray. The leaders sent him a copy of the telephone book. As long as we are ministering to hurting people, we will never lack an audience.

Let it be said, this is not an elective in the Christian life. Jesus, in Matthew 25:34 and following, revealed His priorities in the court of no appeal. Had we been speaking, we would have probably said, "Come, inherit the kingdom prepared for you from the foundation of the world. For you did not drink, smoke, or chew, therefore, we receive you." The Lord Jesus, however, had a different message. "For I was hungry and you gave me something to eat, I was thirsty and you gave me something to drink, I was a stranger and you invited me in, I needed clothes and you clothed me, I was sick and you looked after me, I was in prison and you came to visit me" (Matt. 25:34-36, NIV). Because a Christian is one in whom Christ lives, then His concern becomes our concern and that which breaks His heart, breaks our hearts.

2. Next we see four men with *heart*—the four who came bringing the man to Christ. As far as we know, these men were laymen. There is no suggestion that they were trained theologians. We would do well to learn from this. If we are going to meet the needs of the walking wounded, it is imperative that we mobilize the laity. Too many churches are dying from staff infection. Too many churches rely on paying people to care.

Hope for the Hurting

Several years ago, at Ridgecrest, I was speaking to a group of young seminarians. One of them asked me, "What is the greatest mistake you ever made in the ministry?" For a moment, I had no answer. I've made so many mistakes, how could I possibly single out the greatest? But then God gave me the answer as I gave this young man the answer: "The greatest mistake I ever made was when I had the idea I was the only one in the church who knew how to do anything. The greatest move I ever made was when I loosed laymen to do what God had called them to do." In our church we have 1,400 volunteer positions filled by God's lay people. My task is to equip these saints for the work of the ministry. Note the qualities of these four laymen.

They were men of *compassion*. Tony Campolo, when he spoke in our church, told of a young student addressing a Christian student body. The young man said, "Today and every day 30,000 people die of starvation in this world in which we live. The great tragedy is that most Christians don't give a d___." Then he said, "An even greater tragedy is that when you leave here, you will be more upset that I used that word than you are that 30,000 people died of starvation today." I do not know who originally said it, but they hit the target with pinpoint accuracy when they said, "The world does not care how much we know until they know how much we care."

They were men of *conviction*. These men really believed Jesus was able to meet the needs of this man. The question is, do we believe that? Not only do I believe in the miraculous power of Christ to heal the sick, but I believe in His miraculous power to provide provision for the homeless and the hurting. Often when I share in conferences, the question is asked, "Can we afford this?" That is the wrong question. The question is, "Is it God's will?" And if it is God's will, I assure you He can afford it!

In Leesburg, the miracles of God's provision have been awesome. Recently, we needed $2,000,000 to build our new Christian Care Village. The village, when completed, will include: a Rescue Mission, a Women's Shelter, a Teen Girl's Home, an Emergency Rescue Shelter for Children, a Pregnancy Care Center, a Furniture Barn, a Clothes Closet, and a Food Pantry. I did not want to go into a financial campaign to raise the money. We had just raised $2,000,000 for our Family Life Center, and I wasn't anxious to jump into another campaign. Instead, I shared the vision of the village with our church family, and the Holy Spirit began raising the money.

One lady came forward and said, "I have some land that can be sold and the money used for the village." The land was

Christians in the Public Square

appraised at $820,000. She also said, "I'd like to give some cash." I said, "How much?" She said, "$100,000." Without revealing her name, I shared with the church family what she had done. Shortly thereafter, the Spirit prompted another man to give $100,000. I informed the church family. In a few days, a couple, who were not members of the church, committed $75,000 to the project. I shared that and then said, "The Holy Spirit is raising the money, and we are not going to stifle what He is doing. The last Sunday in October we will give you an opportunity to make a commitment. No one is going to come see you. No one is going to ask you to give. We simply ask that you do what the Holy Spirit prompts you to do." To make a long story short, by the last Sunday in October, more than $2,000,000 was committed. The Holy Spirit miraculously raised the money!

They were men of *creativity*. When they got to the house and saw that it was packed, they were not discouraged. Instead, they went up on the roof, tore a hole in it, and lowered the man down to Jesus. If we are going to reach a lost, hurting world for Jesus Christ, we too must be a people of creativity. Two things are required: (1) We must be willing to do new things; (2) we must be willing to do some of the old things unusually well.

One of the new things that has been a tremendous blessing to our fellowship is Saturday Sunday School. We meet at 10:00 a.m. on Saturday, busing in children and teens. We average more than 300 per Saturday. Many of these children are from destitute situations. It has been awesome to see God's Spirit do such a marvelous work as these children come to a saving knowledge of Christ and begin growing in Him.

One of the old things we do unusually well is a two-week Vacation Bible School each summer. Last year we ministered to 1,300, with more than 50 of them coming to a saving knowledge of the Lord Jesus. We have a volunteer force of more than 300 ministering to these children. Without creativity, without doing new things, without doing old things unusually well, we will never reach hurting people for Christ.

They were men of *cooperation*. Four came, four saw, four cared, four knelt, four carried their shares of the load as they brought the man to Jesus. We sometimes forget that our brother in Christ is not the enemy. The urgency of the hour demands the unity of the church as together we seek a lost and hurting world for Jesus.

3. We see the *hindrance*—the people in the crowd. They did not mean to hinder. They did not intend to be a problem. But, in this case, the four had to go around them to get to Jesus. In every

Hope for the Hurting

community we have the hurting. In every church we have those with heart. But, in every church we also have those who hinder. We have those who stand between Christ and the man in need.

There was a man who was going squirrel hunting. A friend said, "Where are you going?" "I'm going squirrel hunting," was the reply. "Where is your gun?" the friend inquired. "I don't need one," said the hunter. Surprised, the friend asked, "Well, how are you going to kill the squirrels?" The hunter answered, "I'm going to ugly them to death." The friend asked, "How are you going to do that?" The hunter said, "Come with me; I'll show you." Together they went out into the woods. A squirrel ran up the tree and the man and hunter made an ugly face at the squirrel. The squirrel dropped dead. The friend said, "That's amazing! I've never seen anyone who could do that! Is that a family trait? Can others in your family do it?" The hunter replied, "Yes, my mother-in-law can. But we don't let her hunt. She tears up the meat too bad!"

I don't agree with that on mother-in-laws, but I do know a lot of church members who ugly people to death. Many professed Christians do not seem to realize that their conversion is supposed to include their disposition. We will never reach the people we ought to reach for the glory of Christ until we discover what Paul calls the "more excellent way."

If I speak in the tongues of men and of angels, but have not love, I am only a resounding gong or a clanging cymbal. If I have the gift of prophecy and can fathom all mysteries and all knowledge, and if I have a faith that can move mountains, but have not love, I am nothing. If I give all I possess to the poor and surrender my body to the flames, but have not love, I gain nothing (1 Cor. 13:1-3, NIV).

4. We see the *healer*—Jesus, the Christ. I have wonderful news: Jesus is alive and He is well! His church is alive and it is well! And I have discovered that any place will do if God is in the place. And any preacher will do if God is in the preacher. I remember when I was first called to Leesburg. The downtown church, more than 100 years old, had been on the decline for ten years, going from 400 to 300 in Sunday school. They had fired the previous pastor. The congregation was wired together by organization, frozen together by formality, and rusted together by tradition. The first Sunday I was there I decided to warm the service up by asking the people to hold hands and sing "Sweet, Sweet Spirit".

That Sunday afternoon I received a call from a deacon who

Christians in the Public Square

said, "Preacher, we are not going charismatic, are we? That's what Westside did before they went charismatic. Besides, you know what a man is thinking when he holds hands with another man's wife."

The next Sunday, I stood and said, "I'm sorry some were offended when I asked you to hold hands and sing 'Sweet, Sweet Spirit.' I really wasn't being biblical. The Bible doesn't say hold hands, it says, 'Greet each other with a holy kiss.' So, I'd like for you to greet each other with a holy kiss."

The people laughed. They greeted one another with a holy kiss, and a new warmth came on the fellowship. We quickly moved from a high attendance of 300 in August to a high attendance of 600 in October. The church that had averaged 20 baptisms a year baptized more than 100 the next year. This church in the last eight years has averaged almost 300 baptisms a year. We have established over 50 ministries for the hurting. We have been a leader in foreign, home, and state mission giving.

Many would have said, "Nothing significant can happen in a church like First Baptist of Leesburg." But I repeat: Any place will do if God is in the place, and any preacher will do if Christ is in the preacher.

Christ has entrusted a hurting world to our hands. When we look at our hands, what do we see? Do we see busy hands, too busy to reach out to the needy? Do we see dirty hands, too sinful to count for Christ? Do we see delicate hands, too delicate to reach the unkempt? Do we see careless hands, too apathetic to realize our responsibility? I hope not. I pray we will see serving hands coming from a loving heart in which Christ resides.